THE STUDENT'S MUSIC LIBRARY

Edited by Percy M. Young, M.A., Mus.D.

MODERN BRITISH COMPOSERS

In the same series:

THE STUDENT'S MUSIC LIBRARY

MODERN BRITISH COMPOSERS

by

ALAN FRANK

London
DENNIS DOBSON LTD

First published in Great Britain in *MCMLIII* by
DENNIS DOBSON LTD, London. All rights reserved.
Printed in Great Britain by *BRISTOL TYPESETTING
COMPANY*, Stokes Croft, Bristol, 1.
311/R

CONTENTS

INTRODUCTION

THIS IS NOT primarily a book of analysis or criticism, though I hope it will not be found entirely non-critical and undiscriminating. But its purpose is rather to introduce the careers and work (and sometimes their ideas about music) of leading British composers of our own time, presenting them as human beings as well as creative artists. I have attempted to make the essays or portraits informal yet as informative as possible, bearing in mind the particular needs of music teachers and students, especially piano students. Incidentally, is it not one of the inexhaustible joys of music that we who practise it remain students till the end of our days? Where feasible I have laid emphasis on the more approachable and manageable of a composer's works and above all on his piano music; for there can be no better introduction to new music than to play it oneself, or at least grapple with it, at the keyboard. I speak as one brought up to learn his classical symphonies not through radio and gramophone, but through piano solo or duet versions played in the home circle. But this is not to belittle the use of radio and gramophone today, both vital means of dissemination of new music. Recordings, plus if possible an orchestral score, are strongly to be recommended for the study of unfamiliar and often complex works: repetition is what is needed here, and that the gramophone (and only the gramophone) can provide. Fortunately a good deal of modern British music is now recorded, much more than even a few years ago, and details are given at the end of this book.

There are many more British composers today than those I have chosen to discuss here. This book is not, and could not be, comprehensive: I am aware that I have omitted several composers of distinction, a few senior, as well as a number of younger ones. Even though, to paraphrase Belloc, 'my sins (of omission) are scarlet', I hope this book will be read—for what it does contain rather than for what it does not. Surely it is one of the most remarkable and exciting facts of modern musical history that this country should have produced, so soon after Elgar, composers of the calibre of Vaughan Williams, Walton, Britten and Rawsthorne, to mention only the four outstanding ones of those described in this book. It is permissible to ask, without being chauvinistic, whether any other single country can claim so strong a school of twentieth-century composers.

Many of these essays were originally written as a series of articles for *The Music Teacher*. They have been revised for inclusion here, and three further chapters added. I am grateful to my friend Mr J. Raymond Tobin, the Editor of that magazine, for allowing me to make use of this material, for making the suggestion that it should be published in book form, and, not least, for initially encouraging me to write these portraits.

A.F.

Summer, 1953.

I

R. VAUGHAN WILLIAMS

(b. 1872)

RALPH VAUGHAN WILLIAMS celebrated his eight-
ieth birthday on October 12, 1952, and at one of the
several birthday parties which he attended, he remarked that
'being 80' was not a thing he recommended: 'be 79 or 81',
he said, 'but I do advise you all against being 80'. It was a
typical remark, calculated to deflate any formal, deferential
homage that might be paid to our senior composer: there is
nothing that he detests more than gush. Yet it is difficult to
speak with reservation, or without deepest affection, of one
who is so surely a great man as well as a great composer: the
two have not always gone together in musical history.

Of the man, it can, I think, be said that Vaughan Williams
has the true humility that goes with greatness, and that being
so, it follows that he is essentially a human and approachable
person—as any one of the many people who have had occasion to ask his help or advice knows. If you write a letter to
him, you get an answer and usually a quick one (which is
more than can be said for some composers). Up to a little
while ago, he wrote out his letters in his own handwriting:
now he sometimes has them typed for him. If I may obtrude a
personal note, I may add that in recent years I have had to cor-
respond for professional reasons with Vaughan Williams at the
rate of at least one or two letters per week and sometimes more
than one per day. I have never found him other than quick and
efficient in dealing with my often rather tiresome questions.
How—I recently asked someone who knew his household well
—does he manage to find time for such careful attention to cor-
respondence in the midst of all his other labours, which after
all include that of being a not unprolific composer? 'It's be-

cause of his habit', I was told, 'of working before breakfast!'

Another reason, I cannot help feeling, why Vaughan Williams has time to achieve so much is that for many years now he has lived very quietly in Dorking, Surrey, and has refused to get caught up in the time-consuming whirl of metropolitan life of today.[1] That is not to say that he has shut himself away: quite the contrary, for locally he has always been, and still is, a prime mover in amateur musical activities. From the beginning he took the Leith Hill (Dorking) Festival under his wing and wrote his well-known cantata, *Benedicite*, for its twenty-fifth anniversary, in 1930. He still goes from village to village, taking choir rehearsals, and the annual performances which he conducts at Dorking of the *St Matthew Passion* are an unforgettable experience.

No composer in this country has ever understood amateur needs so well or has catered for them so splendidly and with such evident relish. Several of his most recent works are specially designed for amateur use, and this is but one example of how his own natural humility comes out—there is no question of his being 'above' the world of the humblest music-maker. Similarly he himself seeks advice and listens to it: he does not regard his works when written in first (or even second) draft as untouchable. He will always 'try out' new works on friends and from their reactions will often sit down and re-write passages. This has always been his habit and he has paid generous tribute to those who have helped him with criticism. Foremost among these was Gustav Holst, of whom he has written:

I remember after the first orchestral rehearsal of *Job* his almost going on his knees to beg me to cut out some of the percussion with which my inferiority complex had led me to overload the score. Over-scoring has always been one of my vices, and it arises, I am convinced, from the fact that I am not always sure enough of myself and have not the courage of my convictions, and that I must hide my nakedness with an apron of orchestration.

[1] As this book goes to press (Sept. 1953), he is disproving my words by moving to Central London!

These sentences come from an altogether fascinating and entertaining chapter of 'Musical Autobiography' which he wrote for Hubert Foss's book on Vaughan Williams, published by Messrs. Harrap. I warmly commend to readers the whole book and particularly this chapter. They will learn far more about Vaughan Williams from it than from any dull recitation of biographical data which I could produce here. Vaughan Williams writes especially of his early musical upbringing. Indeed he deals with his very first composition, no longer extant. It was a four-bar piano piece written when he was six and called, for no apparent reason, *The Robin's Nest*. Attempts were made to teach him the piano, but he could never get to grips with it, which is possibly one reason why he has not written very much for this instrument (but he admits that he invariably uses the piano when composing, a practice which certain superior composers regard with scorn.) At a preparatory school at Rottingdean he fared better with the violin, playing Raff's *Cavatina* at a school concert. 'Fifty years later', he writes, 'at one of the Three Choirs' Festivals, I was suddenly moved to seize W. H. Reed's violin and play through Raff's *Cavatina* by heart, double stops and all, while Reed vamped an accompaniment before a discerning and enthusiastic audience.' He tells too of his training at the Royal College of Music, first under Parry and then Stanford ('a great teacher, but I believe I was unteachable'); and of his first appointment as organist, at a church in South Lambeth. This was, as it happens, also his last appointment, for he was no better on the organ than on the piano. None the less, since he had to take the choir and accompany services, he gained there insight into the choice and practical use of church music, which was to prove of the greatest value in his later years, when he was to undertake the editing of such publications as *The English Hymnal* and *Songs of Praise*.

Vaughan Williams has strong likes and dislikes in music, and gives honest—even blunt—expression to them, at times shocking the susceptibilities of others. For example, many feel (I do myself) that his opinion of Mahler, whom he has described as a 'tolerable imitation of a composer', is quite outrageous. Vaughan Williams seems indeed to have something of an obsessive dislike of this composer, which has its entertaining side. He once asked me to obtain for him (a) some examples of atonal compositions—'the wrong-note school', and (b) a score of Mahler's *Resurrection Symphony*, which for some reason he wished to study: 'not for its wrong notes', he wrote: 'they all seem painfully right to me.'

Beethoven, too, he used to dislike and he writes, in the same chapter from which I hope I have quoted enough to send the reader straight to it:

To this day the Beethoven idiom repels me, but I hope I have at last learnt to see the greatness that lies behind the idiom that I dislike, and at the same time to see an occasional weakness behind the Bach idiom which I love.

On the subject of Bach performance today, Vaughan Williams holds determined views, and a remarkable broadcast talk on the occasion of the Bach bicentenary, entitled 'Bach, the Great Bourgeois', gave certain scholars some severe jolts. Vaughan Williams does not approve of the movement to 'play Bach as he wrote it', pointing out that we cannot do so even if we want to. And to the question 'Do we want to?' Vaughan Williams answers an emphatic 'No'. 'Why should we perform Bach with all the disabilities under which he suffered any more than we perform Shakespeare in the Elizabethan pronunciation? . . . "The letter killeth but the spirit giveth life." If we adhere meticulously and mechanically to the letter of Bach we shall inevitably kill the spirit.'

Similarly I believe that Vaughan Williams would deprecate an over-reverent attitude towards the 'letter' of his own notes and markings. Even in his concert works he has always been willing—sometimes too willing—to sanction some slight deviation from the printed score if the performer can make a valid case for doing so. When it comes to works for amateurs, Vaughan Williams himself often allows for considerable latitude or adaptation in their execution. One example is the *Household Music* (revealing title), which though written for string quartet can alternatively be played on a variety of instruments, including recorders, euphonium, saxhorn, cornet, saxophones, parts being provided. A rather different example of a work in which all can join in is his *Concerto Grosso*, written in 1950 for the twenty-first anniversary of the Rural Music Schools and performed under Sir Adrian Boult by their massed orchestra at the Albert Hall. This work is laid out for four groups of string players: (a) players of professional or near-professional ability, (b) good amateurs, (c) not-so-good amateurs, (d) the duffers, who play on open strings only.

Two recent occasional pieces for choirs are his cantata, *The Sons of Light*, and *Folk Songs of the Four Seasons*, written respectively for the Schools Music Association of Great Britain and the National Federation of Women's Institutes. Both of them were also heard for the first time at the Albert Hall, under the auspices of these organisations. *The Sons of Light*, a setting of a vivid poem by Ursula Wood, is quite a tough nut, yet the S.A.T.B. contingents recruited from the schools encompassed it without strain and with complete conviction at its first performance. *Folk Songs of the Four Seasons*, a godsend for women's choirs, consists of some fifteen settings, three or four for each of the seasons of the year, written variously in one, two, three or four parts, and using semi-chorus as well as full chorus. Winter comes last and the final setting is a most stirring one of the Sussex Mummers' Carol, 'God Bless the Master of this House'.

In all these works, while there is an easing of technical problems, there is none the less no sign of writing down: musically they are entirely characteristic.

Two other choral works, for mixed choirs, may be mentioned here together, because both are based on operas. There is the well-known cantata *In Windsor Forest*, the music adapted from the Shakespearian opera, *Sir John in Love*: and recently the cantata entitled *A Cotswold Romance* has appeared, adapted by Maurice Jacobson in collaboration with the composer, from the romantic ballad opera, *Hugh the Drover*. This is a far longer work, of some ten numbers, needing tenor and soprano soli. It includes the famous boxing match scene between Hugh and John the Butcher, for a stake of £20.

I have already mentioned that Vaughan Williams has written relatively little for the piano, though there is a Piano Concerto (also for two pianos and orchestra), and a fairly new work, *Fantasia on the Old 104th Psalm Tune,* laid out for the unusual forces of solo piano, accompanied by chorus and orchestra. There are two short pieces for piano solo worthy of attention. One is the *Hymn Tune Prelude* on the beautiful 'Song 13' by Orlando Gibbons, a very playable piece. Rather more difficult, but still manageable, is *The Lake in the Mountains,* based on music written for the film 49*th Parallel.*

This was Vaughan Williams's first film score, undertaken (to everyone's surprise) when he was nearly seventy. From it, too, comes the tune which is so widely sung in its many arrangements, *The New Commonwealth.* Subsequently Vaughan Williams has written the scores of some half dozen films, including a year or two ago, *Scott of the Antarctic.*

In addition to the works already discussed there is at least as much again in his output about which I could write, for he has composed steadily in most categories, piano and chamber music least. In the symphonic field alone, there are seven works, ranging from the *Sea Symphony* of 1905-10 to the *Sinfonia Antartica* of 1953, as well as *Job,* which can almost be reckoned as another symphony. There is the fairly early Tallis *Fantasia for Double String Orchestra,* intensely moving in its restraint, and in the repertoire of most of the orchestras of the world. There are the operas, notably of course *Pilgrim's Progress,* a consummate expression of the composer's long pre-occupation with Bunyan's classic. At the other end of the scale in size, but of no less importance in appraising his influence on our musical experience, are the numerous arrangements of English folk songs and carols, to the collecting and setting of which he has devoted a major part of his working life.

What next? Another opera or symphony, or—just as likely—something quite unpredictable? That he is working—and with undiminished powers—is known. May he never run out of manuscript paper!

II

JOHN IRELAND

(b. 1879)

JOHN IRELAND is seven years younger than Vaughan Williams. Both composers have played notable parts during the last forty or so years in the very striking twentieth-century renaissance of British music. There is a difference between the contributions made to it by these two men. As I have pointed out in the previous chapter, Vaughan Williams is rather an unpredictable composer, having given us many surprises and being still something of an adventurer in his music. John Ireland, in contrast, established early in his career a personal style and has maintained it consistently through the years, such development as has taken place in his music having been devoted to the technical perfecting of this style. He has remained an incurable and unashamed romantic —together with his pupil, the late E. J. Moeran, and Sir Arnold Bax, Ireland is at the head of what may be called the modern romantic school of British composition. Ireland has occasionally been criticised for 'not keeping abreast with the times', but the criticism is surely a mistaken one. He has resolutely refused—and one respects him for it—to be deflected by transient idiomatic fashions from writing the music which is the real expression of his temperament: consequently his music sounds *less* dated than many a smart quip which appeared so up-to-date in the 1920's.

I have said that Ireland is a romantic composer, but there is nothing mushy or nebulous about his music. It is clear-cut and disciplined, and his evocation of moods is brought about by firm musical invention. In this respect his writing has precision similar to that of Debussy or Ravel, both of whom have had some influence on him, for example in the use of

15

decorative arabesque in his piano writing, and, especially Ravel, in his harmonic procedure.

The reader will find that several of the modern British composers discussed in this book have written very little indeed for the piano, or, where they have done so, piano music cannot be said to be an important part of their total output. In the case of Ireland, however, himself a fine and sensitive pianist, the reverse is true: his piano music, especially the considerable number of shortish lyrical pieces, must be reckoned not only as Ireland's most valuable contribution to modern English music, but also as an outstanding addition to European piano literature of today. This implies no disrespect for, or lack of appreciation of, his achievement in other fields, notably the solo song. But in the piano category Ireland is a major exponent of a minor *genre*. The use of the word 'minor' must not be misunderstood: we have only to think of the short piano pieces of Schumann and Grieg to realise that perfect works of art are just as likely to be found in smaller, unpretentious shapes, as when they are written on a massive scale. The mediums which Grieg favoured are indeed very comparable to those which have appealed to John Ireland—in either case the bulk of their output consists of piano pieces, songs, a smaller amount of chamber music, and only one concerto: Grieg wrote no symphony, nor, so far, has Ireland. Since I have mentioned the particular attention which Ireland has paid to the piano, it is worth noting that his chamber music invariably includes a piano, and thus he has not written a string quartet.

Before passing on to my particular purpose of reviewing John Ireland's music for piano solo, a few brief details of his life and career may be given. There is in fact not a great deal to say because, in the words of the writer in *Grove's Dictionary*, his life has remained 'outwardly uneventful'. He comes from Cheshire, and both his mother and father had literary gifts—his father being Editor of the *Manchester Examiner*. Books formed, then, the background of his early days, and eminent writers such as Carlyle, Emerson and Leigh Hunt were friends of his parents. It is not surprising, because of this literary background, that in later life Ireland's choice of poems for setting to music reveals a fine taste, and that the literary quotations which frequently prefix his piano pieces exhibit a wide reading. Towards the end of last century, Ireland became a student of the Royal College of Music and, like a great number of contemporary English composers, he studied under Stanford. Subsequently he himself became one of the most distinguished professors of composition at the Royal College (Benjamin Britten was one of his pupils).

Ireland has spent a good deal of his life either in the Channel Islands (which he first visited about forty years ago, and in which he was living up to the time of their invasion by the Germans in the last war) or in London, more specifically Chelsea. Both these regions have had influence on the subject matter of his music, as will be seen. In appearance, there is nothing of the aesthete about him—he might well be mistaken for a family solicitor in a country town, or perhaps a bank manager telling you—kindly, with barely a hint of punitive measures—that you have an overdraft. He is, and has always been, rather a recluse, yet he numbers among his most intimate friends some of his very well-known colleagues in English composition, such as Arnold Bax, William Walton and Alan Rawsthorne.

At a guess, there are something like fifty pieces for piano solo by him. Most of them were written between the years 1913-1921. Among the earliest are his only pieces which can be described as strictly educational music. These are *Three Dances—Country Dance, Gipsy Dance* and *Reapers' Dance*—they are lively and good of their type, but not in the least characteristic: the first might be by Edward German.

Much more interesting are a number of pieces which can be graded as 'moderately easy' and can thus be tackled by students of modest attainments. Yet they contain some of his very best pieces. My own favourite among them is *The Darkened Valley,* prefaced by a quotation from Blake, 'Walking along the darkened valley, With silent melancholy'. In this piece, perhaps more than in any other, the influence of Ravel

B

is to be found. The writing is clear and economic, and the whole piece has an outstandingly attractive flow. Other pieces of about the same difficulty include the rather better-known *The Holy Boy*, from a set of Four Preludes. This shows Ireland in a characteristic mood of utter simplicity, such as he also attained in a notable song—his setting of Christina Rossetti's *When I am Dead*. Not dissimilar in its simple, limpid mood is the piece entitled *Soliloquy*. *The Towing Path*, inscribed 'Pangbourne 1918', is a gentle sustained six-eight piece, rather resembling the more difficult and familiar *Chelsea Reach*. Other titles which may just be noted as coming in this fairly easy category are *Month's Mind*, *Summer Evening*, *Cypress* (from a set of pieces called *Greenways*—the Shakespearian quotation 'Come away, come away death, And in sad cypress let me be laid' gives the clue to the mood of the piece) and *A Grecian Lad*, which carries a quotation from Housman's *A Shropshire Lad*. Incidentally, according to an essay by the late Ralph Hill,[1] it seems that the majority of these titles and quotations have been added by Ireland after the music was written, so as to induce in listener and performer an approximation to the intended mood.

In the next grade of difficulty come several of his best-known pieces, and, particularly because they are written and laid out so expertly for the piano, they are not of excessive difficulty. *Chelsea Reach*, for example, the first of his *Three London Pieces*, and the most popular of all his piano pieces, in the grateful key of A flat lies beautifully under the fingers, especially if one has a reasonably wide stretch. The other two most attractive pieces in the set are *Ragamuffin*, which needs a light, crisp touch, and the rather more difficult *Soho Forenoons*. Hardly less well known in this grade is the piece *April*, which was recorded by the composer. Ireland's style is often warmly chromatic in its chordal aspect, and this can be seen very typically in the expressive smooth piece, *For Remembrance*, in the key of E flat, rather a favourite key

[1] In *British Music of our Time*, published by Pelican Books, to which the reader is recommended for further detail.

of his for pieces of this type. *Spring Will Not Wait* also has a quotation from Housman, and shows Ireland in a mood of nostalgic melancholy—many of his pieces can be classed as either being in this highly personal mood, or in complete contrast to it, namely a mood of brisk, uninhibited vigour, often in two-two time.

Two really difficult sets of pieces have interest, as they partly owe their inspiration to the Channel Islands. The first piece of the set entitled *Decorations* is inscribed 'Fauvic, Jersey, August, 1912', and its self-explanatory title is *The Island Spell*. Its special tonal effects call for constant and very exact use of the sustaining pedal, and it has a curious, somewhat mysterious atmosphere. The later set is called *Sarnia*, which was the name given by the Romans to the island of Guernsey. It is his most recent major work for piano solo, though written about twelve years ago. It consists of a sequence of three pieces, each dedicated to a Channel Islander: the first piece bears the title *Le Catioroc*, which is the name of a coastal region of Guernsey, where it seems there is—or was until recently—still trace of prehistoric nature-worship being carried out; *In a May Morning* opens relatively easily, and throughout is the least difficult of the three pieces; and the last is *Song of the Springtides*, a buoyant piece for the virtuoso.

Of the two formally titled works for piano, the highly individual Sonatina, perhaps the more playable of the two, attracts me more than the Sonata. Its first two movements contain music of great depth, which grows on one the more one plays it. The final rondo is a thoroughly extrovert, brilliant piece, which was chosen years before the war as a test piece in a competition for piano playing organised by *The Daily Express*, the competition being won by the young Mr Cyril Smith. Other pieces to be mentioned among Ireland's difficult music include the well-known and charmingly flowing *Amberley Wild Brooks*; and brisk pieces such as *Merry Andrew, Puck's Birthday,* and *Bergomask*. This last demands skilful dynamic control by the fingers, since its tune is in the middle part, played by the right hand, which must also contrive simultaneously to fill in the harmony above it.

No discussion of Ireland's contribution to piano literature could be complete without reference to his Piano Concerto, first performed in 1930, and subsequently recorded with Eileen Joyce as soloist. The breadth and grace of the first movement, and the simple warmth of the slow movement which recurs in the course of the otherwise gay finale, make this one of the most justly popular piano concertos of today. Equally popular and also recorded is his *London Overture,* and recent gramophone issues under the auspices of the British Council include his two descriptive tone poems, *Mai-Dun* and *The Forgotten Rite.* It may be appropriate to mention that both these orchestral works are also available in piano duet versions.

During the twentieth century, the modern composer has often been accused of drawing away from the public, of becoming too intellectual, recondite and abstract to have any real contact with the bulk of listeners or performers. This is strikingly untrue of John Ireland, who, without any sacrifice of musical integrity, has attained over the years a genuine popularity, unshaken by ephemeral fashion. Above all it is the pianist, amateur and professional alike, who is indebted to him as to no other living English composer.

III

SIR ARNOLD BAX

(b. 1883)[1]

IF YOU LOOK up the name of Sir Arnold Bax in a dictionary of music, you will almost certainly find that no more than a few laconic lines are devoted to the biographical side of his life. If you question Bax himself on the subject, I am sure you would get an equally laconic answer from this most reserved musician, as shy at nearly seventy as he was when a youth. The facts are that he was born in London in 1883, three years before his equally distinguished brother Clifford, the poet and dramatist; he entered the Royal Academy of Music in 1900; he has lived and travelled in (besides England), Ireland, Scotland and Russia; he was knighted in 1937, until 1942 held no official position—the faintest suggestion of limelight makes him shyer than ever —but in that year, following the death of Sir Walford Davies, he was appointed Master of the King's Musick.

But there is more to it than these unadorned facts suggest, as was made delightfully evident in 1943 when Bax published some memoirs of his early life, up to the beginning of the 1914-18 war. This book, entitled *Farewell, My Youth*[2] is one which readers may well have missed on its wartime appearance. I did myself and, reading it only recently, found it one of the most enjoyable, entertaining, and admirably written books by any native musician of today that has come my way. Because, furthermore, it is now out of print (but can and should be tracked down in your public library) I make no apology for drawing quite heavily on it in the course of

[1] As this book goes to press we learn with regret of the death of Sir Arnold Bax on October 3rd, 1953.

[2] Longmans Green.

21

this article. It reveals, among other things, a quality of decidedly caustic wit, with perhaps an occasional tiniest tinge of malice, that I for one had not realised existed in Bax, from a merely casual acquaintance with him.

The Bax family comes of Surrey stock, his ancestors having held land in the Dorking-Leith Hill area. Bax himself was born not exactly in what we now know as Surrey, but in the South London suburb of Streatham, which in the 1880s still possessed, he writes, 'a certain mellowness and port-wininess about some of the older streets'. Of his early days he writes: 'I cannot remember a time when I had not the same miserable smattering of French which is all I can muster now, and similarly I cannot recall the long lost day when I was unable to play the piano,' reading music as easily as most people read a book. The acquiring of foreign languages is evidently not one of Bax's accomplishments, for from his later extended visits to Russia, he admits that he learnt only sufficient Russian to get him through the scoring and technical terms of billiards, a game which—like cricket—has always been one of his delights.

His father, reasonably prosperous, was not unmusical, and his uncle was an accredited music critic of a London evening paper, while knowing little of the technique of music: nothing unusual in that, Bax suggests, even today. Shortly before the end of the century, the family moved north of the river, to Hampstead. 'Art was certainly rampant on the northern heights' at that time, and at the Town Hall Bax used to hear the Joachim Quartet, 'with the old man frequently apt to play just out of tune'. Piano and violin lessons, together with cricket, occupied a good deal of his time, and in 1898 he became a student at the Hampstead Conservatoire, at whose head was Cecil Sharp, later to become celebrated throughout the world. It is worth noting that Bax neither had, nor has, any enthusiasm at all for the folk song and dance movement, and expressed himself acidly on this point. It is also worth mentioning that, despite his burning interest in Celtic art, only once in his composing career has he made use of an actual folk song.

When he entered the Royal Academy of Music, then in Tenterden Street off Oxford Street, he found as fellow students musicians such as Eric Coates, York Bowen, Stanley Marchant, Adam Carse, and later 'two very small and eternally giggling girls', Myra Hess and Irene Scharrer. In those days Wagner and Strauss were the composers that fascinated him, for it was not until his student days were virtually ended that Debussy came to be known in England. Many co-students of Bax's at the Academy have testified to his phenomenal skill and quickness at reading full scores at the piano. Otherwise, he says that he made little mark as a student and was slow to develop, and had to work hard to gain any technical facility in composition. One of the earliest performances of a work of his that he recalls was of a set of Symphonic Variations done at a Patrons' Fund rehearsal at the Royal College of Music. To his astonishment and horror Bax was instructed at the very last minute to conduct the work, and he there and then decided that never again would he direct his own work in public, from which resolution he has never deviated.

His preoccupation with late nineteenth-century German romanticism was not really thrown off until, in a vivid flash, he discovered the innate feeling within him for Celticism through reading the work of W. B. Yeats. Bax acknowledges his great debt to Yeats in the warmest terms, and he was still under twenty when he made his way to Yeats's country for the first time. Subsequently he spent many years in Ireland, and in the earlier part of this century found happiness and content there which he has barely experienced elsewhere. Like Moeran, he was above all fascinated by the West Coast, especially the north-west, around Donegal, 'that sea-fretted edge of Europe', to use his own graphic phrase. Here he began to write verses and stories based on Irish subjects, published under the pseudonym of Dermot O'Byrne. Often, in fact, he actually wrote his stories in the exact and usually remote location on the West Coast where their plots were set. Generally at this period he was dividing his time between music and literature—as well as playing cards with his Irish neighbour friends on the kitchen table of the inn where he used to stay.

When the first world war broke out, Bax was just in his thirties: it is at this point, if we take his book of memoirs literally, that he said farewell to his youth. He had already written a good deal of music in most forms, and his prolific-ness was to be continued, and even increased, in the period between the two wars. It was then—from 1922 to 1939—that the rich, yet frequently sombre, series of no less than seven symphonies appeared. It is remarkable that three of these had their first performance not in this country, but in America, somewhat surprisingly since one hardly thinks of Bax's music as being markedly exportable: or at least it is less obviously exportable than the music of some of his colleagues. However that may be, the Second Symphony, dedicated to Koussevitsky, was first given by him at Boston in 1929, the Fourth in San Francisco under Basil Cameron three years later, and the Seventh was first heard in New York under the auspices of the British Council in 1939, con-ducted by Sir Adrian Boult. Today the symphonies of Bax are none too often heard, partly because of their difficulty in execution. One of them, however—the Third—in many ways the finest, is recorded by the Hallé Orchestra under Barbirolli. Also there is a most interesting analysis of this particular symphony, written from the viewpoint of a most distinguished orchestral player, in *Sixteen Symphonies*,[1] by Bernard Shore, for a long time principal viola player of the B.B.C. Symphony Orchestra. Fairly frequently heard, its genial and dashing moods forming a contrast with the more darkly coloured aspect of the symphonies, is the *Overture to a Picaresque Comedy*, which was also recorded, under the late Sir Hamilton Harty to whom it was dedicated. Of his more picturesque programmatic music, two works are outstanding, both dating from his early thirties, *The Garden of Fand* and *Tintagel*, the former recorded under Beecham and recently used as a ballet. A good deal of Bax's music has a programme to it—even the Fourth Symphony is admitted by the composer to be

[1] Longmans Green.

in part 'nature music'—but he has made it clear that his music ought to be explicit on its own, without the listener necessarily knowing the programme, literary or otherwise, behind it.

I have already mentioned that, from his very earliest days, Bax was completely at home at the keyboard, and was a phenomenal sight-reader. It is to be expected, therefore, that he has written a good deal of piano music, both solo and for two pianos, and piano and orchestra. For the most part it is, though expertly written, difficult music for the player, rather more difficult, say, than the comparable piano pieces by John Ireland: these two among English composers are alone responsible for a very high proportion of lyrical piano music produced in this country during the twentieth century. One of the simplest of about a dozen short pieces which Bax has written for piano solo is his *Country Tune*, but even this has its traps. It is a most attractive *allegretto* tune, with a quicker middle section which presents a high staccato theme of a pipe-like nature. Bax frequently transfers melodic interest to the left hand, giving the right hand the accompaniment figure, often of a rippling nature: it occurs at times in this *Country Tune*, and also in other pieces which are at least manageable by a reasonably fluent pianist—*A Hill Tune* and *A Lullaby* (Berceuse). A piece of Bax's which, though originally written for piano, has become popular in other forms, is that entitled *Mediterranean*, known both as an orchestral work and in a violin arrangement by Heifetz. It is a warm and languorous evocation of the southern climate, and a most grateful piece to play. Of a quite different nature, as different as north is from south, is a set of Variations on a North Country Christmas Carol 'O Dame get up and bake your pies'. This carries the dedication: 'To Anna and Julian Herbage, in acknowledgment of pies baked and enjoyed " on Christmas Day in the Morning," 1945'. Other fairly playable pieces of his which need to be mentioned include a *Ceremonial Dance* in minuet time, with a contrasted quicker section, characteristic of one side of Bax and marked 'hard and dry'; and a *Burlesque*, dedicated to Iso Elinson, which, however, may well have to be played rather slower than its metronome mark to be manageable. For piano solo there are also two lyrical pieces taken from the film score which Bax wrote for *Oliver Twist*: they are quite straightforward and pleasant, though not especially distinguished.

A major contribution to piano literature is comprised by his four Piano Sonatas, the first of which was written during a summer spent in the Ukraine in 1910, and the latest of which dates from some twenty-five years later, having been first performed in New York by Miss Harriet Cohen. They are all difficult works and essentially romantic works: the fourth, however, is the most concisely written, and therefore the most playable. It is also to me the finest of them, and especially the slow movement, built on an almost continuous pedal on G sharp, is one of Bax's most beautiful pieces in this vein (an opinion which is apparently shared by the composer).

No English composer of this century could wish for a more sympathetic and convincing exponent than Bax has had in the person of Miss Harriet Cohen. It is well known that when, a few years ago, Miss Cohen seriously injured her right hand (now happily recovered) Arnold Bax wrote for her a *Concertante for Left Hand and Orchestra.* It was first heard at the Cheltenham Festival of 1950: it is an entirely successful work, and one of the most inventive among his recent output. Critics who in the past have found, not without some justification, that Bax's music in general contains too many notes, were quick to suggest, somewhat caustically, that the exercise of writing for one hand only had resulted in a salutary economy. The slow movement, a touching and—for Bax—surprisingly simple piece, is also available in a normal two-hand piano solo version.

Also asssociated with Miss Harriet Cohen, and recorded by her, is another work for piano and orchestra, on a slight scale but of considerable charm. This is the *Morning Song,* written in 1947 and dedicated to Princess Elizabeth, as she then was. It has the sub-title 'Maytime in Sussex', and is thus a reminder that this is the county where for some years Bax has lived, in the village of Storrington. If latterly he has written rather less music than he used to, he has by his total output up to date enriched English music in all fields, except opera. This chapter would need to be considerably extended were it to deal with his many chamber works, the group of two-piano works, all written for those pioneers of two-piano playing, Ethel and Rae Robertson, his notable songs and choral works. In these as in all his music Bax is a romantic composer—as he himself has put it, 'a brazen romantic, by which I mean that my music is the expression of emotional states. I have no interest whatever in sound for its own sake or in any modernist 'isms or factions.' It is a fair statement.

IV

SIR ARTHUR BLISS

(b. 1891)

IT DOES NOT seem so very long ago—though it is, in mathematical fact, thirty years since the stridently gay 1920s were with us—that Arthur Bliss was one of the youngest and most daring English composers to emerge in those post- (first) war years. There was much of the *enfant terrible* about him then, a somewhat Stravinskian figure who aroused fanatical enthusiasm among the elect advance guard, and distrust among the more staid. It is a sobering thought that this controversial figure is now in his sixties, and is one of the most respected musicians in this country. His music has lost some of its early shock-power, but in turn has acquired a ripe and warm humanity. It has grown up. But Bliss himself, despite greying hair, does not make it any easier for one to remember that he is over sixty. He still has undiminished vigour and high spirits, and a great capacity for enjoying life. He is a remarkably well-preserved man and shows no apparent sign of the fact that he was wounded at the Battle of the Somme and gassed at Cambrai.

Bliss was born in London, and I think of him very much as an urbane, well-dressed and civilised Londoner: I associate him with Hampstead, where he lived for years, with Kensington where he now lives, and with the Savile Club where he is thoroughly at home and a well-liked member. But in fact I get the impression that latterly he has been spending more and more time away from London, at his Somerset home. He has not always been tied to London or even to England. For several years between the two wars he lived in America, and it may be mentioned here that his wife is American, a most attractive personality and a gifted

28

author. Of their two daughters, one is an actress and the other dances in the Sadler's Wells Ballet Company (note the connection with the theatre, of which we shall have more to say in relation to Bliss *père*).

Arthur Bliss is a man of wide contemporary culture, stretching beyond music. And, unlike most composers, he is gifted with a clear, organising brain. Had he not been a composer one can think of many spheres in which he could not have failed to make a success. Even though composition rightly occupies the major part of his life, Bliss has, being a man with a sense of responsibility and of public service, undertaken other activities. At the present time he holds, for example, two important honorary positions. He is, firstly, an admirable Chairman of the Music Advisory Committee of the British Council, and, secondly, Vice-Chairman of the Board of Directors of the Performing Right Society (a remarkable and complex organisation which deals with the collecting and distributing of fees on performances of copyright music and thus provides a major portion of the livelihood of composers and publishers). He has in the past been a Professor of Composition both at the Royal Academy and Royal College of Music, but teaches no longer.

As for Bliss's own studies, he worked at Cambridge University under Charles Wood and took his Mus. B. degree in 1913. He then went to the Royal College under Stanford. His work there was interrupted by the 1914-18 war, throughout which he served in the Army (he took a commission in the Grenadier Guards) and was mentioned in despatches. While on active service two early chamber works were performed and both were published. It says a lot for Bliss's integrity and self-criticism that, after being demobilised, he felt so dissatisfied with these two works that he had the engraved plates and all existing copies destroyed. Young composers are usually too excited at seeing their work in print to take action as drastic as this!

Bliss's real composing career started with a group of works written soon after the 1914-18 war: these include *Madam Noy* for voice and six instruments, and a *Rhapsody* for two voices and seven instruments; the voices in the latter are themselves used as instruments, vocalising on the syllable 'Ah'. The third work of this group is called *Rout*, also using a wordless voice with a small instrumental ensemble. All three works were experimental studies in striking sonorities. They were influenced by Stravinsky, and earned Bliss the reputation, to which I have referred, of being something of an *enfant terrible*. His more substantial *Colour Symphony* of 1922 brought his name before a wider public.

In 1923 he paid his first visit to America and married two years later. Returning to England towards the end of the 1920s, he started on the second and continuing phase of his distinguished career as a composer, the preoccupation with adventure having changed to a more thoughtful and more romantic outlook. But the healthy exuberant spirit was still there and is still evident today. Bliss was in America again at the beginning of the second world war, but he returned to England soon after it began and joined the B.B.C. He became Music Director there in 1942 and remained for three years. Though he filled this post with great accomplishment, I do not think that he was happy as a desk-bound administrator. He may by then have been already contemplating the composition of his first opera *The Olympians*, with libretto by J. B. Priestley, which was produced at Covent Garden in the autumn of 1949. Since then his most outstanding work is his Second String Quartet, dedicated to the Griller Quartet, who gave the first performance of it at the Edinburgh Festival in September, 1950, three months after he received his knighthood in the King's Birthday Honours List. It has been issued by Decca on a long-playing record, performed by these artists.

Let us now go back over some of the notable series of works Arthur Bliss has written in the last twenty-five years. It must be said at once that he has produced regrettably little easy music which can be recommended to amateur performers: also that he has written only a small amount for piano,[1]

[1] Among the few early piano solo works, a set of *Masks* is available, but they are difficult pieces and I do not find them especially rewarding or characteristic of the later Bliss.

rather surprisingly, since he thoroughly understands the keyboard (see, for example, his brilliant exploitation in the solo part of his Piano Concerto) and he himself plays reasonably well. But despite the dearth of music which one can comfortably play for one's own entertainment, the student is fortunately able to get to terms with much of Bliss's output through the gramophone, for several of his more important works are recorded: these include the Piano Concerto just mentioned, the two String Quartets, the Quintet for Clarinet and Strings, the Viola Sonata, *Pastoral,* and much of his ballet and film music.

This list is rather revealing, since it is almost all chamber or orchestral music. From about 1920 to 1940 Bliss wrote very little indeed for the voice, especially little for the solo voice. To choral writing he was more drawn, and two major works are the *Pastoral* ('Lie Strewn the White Flocks') of 1929, and *Morning Heroes,* for orator, chorus and orchestra, of a year later. Of these two works, the former attempts less and is probably the more successful. Indeed it is quite one of Bliss's most attractive and gracious works, and the choral writing is not of excessive difficulty. It is written for mixed voice chorus, optional mezzo-soprano solo, flute, drums and strings. The poems here set are mostly lesser-known and show the range of Bliss's literary taste. They are described as a 'little anthology of bucolic verse', and the poets include the sixteenth-century Ben Jonson and John Fletcher, translated extracts from Poliziano and Theocritus, and two poems by the modern English poet, the late Robert Nichols, who was a friend of Bliss's and indeed of many modern English composers. The work was dedicated to Elgar, a dedication of some interest, because although this particular work has little Elgarian flavour, his later music has shown a distinct influence of Elgar, even though Bliss's has more edge to it. This *Pastoral* has recently been recorded under Dr Reginald Jacques, with Nancy Evans as soloist, a most welcome issue.

I should mention that since 1940, the date of Bliss's excellent *Seven American Poems* for voice and piano—certainly his best songs to date—Bliss shows signs of being more attracted to vocal, as distinct from purely instrumental, writing. The opera *The Olympians* of course was one such sign, and his latest completed work[1] is a Scena for contralto and orchestra entitled *The Enchantress*, an exciting dramatic piece of writing.

Turning to the piano, I have already referred to his Piano Concerto, which is undoubtedly one of his biggest and most important works and also one of his best-known. It is yet another example of Bliss's association with America, for it was commissioned by the British Council for performance at the New York World Fair of 1939, where Solomon was its soloist (and is also the soloist in the older recording). It is dedicated to the people of the United States, and bearing in mind the occasion, it is not surprising that it is a quite deliberate exhibition work, big and expansive, with a tremendous solo part. Its first movement is especially attractive thematically: the finale is sheer brilliance all the way, while there is relief in the tender and warm slow movement. The simple opening, a dialogue between the piano solo and orchestra, of this slow movement, is a memorable and most affecting passage.

An equally well-known work, and an equally lively one, is the *Music for Strings*, which was first heard at Salzburg in 1935. It is an elaborate work, possibly too elaborate: it is a valid criticism that the inner parts are too incessantly packed with incident, and a certain restlessness results.

In the field of chamber music, there are some notable achievements from Bliss's pen. There are the two String Quartets of 1941 and 1950, both recorded by the Griller Quartet. The first Quartet was produced in America where it was played by the Pro Arte String Quartet. The second one has an astonishingly effective and taking Scherzo, and the whole work is full of invention. It is a difficult work, in its different way as much of a show piece for a string quartet as the Piano Concerto is for a solo pianist. Two other chamber works call for mention, both written in the early 30s—

---

[1] Since these words were written a new Piano Sonata has been heard.

the Clarinet Quintet, a beautifully written composition with a fluency about it that is almost Mendelssohnian; and a Viola Sonata written for the great English viola player Lionel Tertis.

Throughout Bliss's music, serious though it is, there is more than a streak of rhetoric and of theatricality. It is no wonder, then, that he is drawn to theatre and film music. Even if *The Olympians* was not quite the unqualified success for which we had hoped, it none the less presents a rich evening's entertainment, and its faults reside less in the composer's share of the work than in its other aspects. The opera ran into some criticism, but if it is true, as it is rumoured, that—nothing daunted—Bliss is engaged on a second opera, that is the best news possible: for undoubtedly Bliss has all the attributes, including a very marked stage sense, to enable him to produce an outstanding opera.

He has written three ballets: *Checkmate,* which was written for the official visit of the Sadler's Wells Ballet to Paris in 1937, *Miracle in the Gorbals* and *Adam Zero,* also produced by the Sadler's Wells Ballet in 1944 and 1946 respectively. All three were first conducted by the late Constant Lambert. Of them, the music which best stands on its own feet is *Checkmate,* and the Suite of Dances from it is popular in the concert hall and in Robert Irving's recording. Of his film music, one score also has found popularity in concert form. It was, in fact, among the earliest film music to interest the concert-goer, apart from its use in the film. This was the music to H. G. Wells's film, *Things to Come,* and attractive numbers in the Suite are the Ballet for Children, the reconstruction theme, and the final March which, stirring piece that it is, has reached an enormously wide public. *Things to Come* was made in 1935. Ten years later Bliss wrote the music to another feature film, *Men of Two Worlds,* and the score is of interest as it includes a miniature Piano Concerto, the piano part of which was played on the sound track by Eileen Joyce.

In reading and hearing again the various works of Arthur Bliss for the purpose of preparing this survey, I found myself

C

impressed equally by the terrific spirit and punch of the fast movements (*con spirito* and *con brio* are markings frequently to be encountered in these movements) and the romantic yet virile warmth of the slower movements. Altogether Bliss's music is full-blooded and exuberant, and ornamented sometimes to the point of lushness. These are qualities that make for popularity: on the technical side, Bliss gains musicians' respect by his enormous technical, and especially contrapuntal, dexterity and aplomb. He tends to over-score rather than the reverse. Today I think we have gone too far in our worship of conciseness and economy, of antiseptic bareness in art. I own that I find Arthur Bliss, precisely because he is so signally lacking in these really not very comforting qualities, a refreshingly human personality in English music.

V

ARTHUR BENJAMIN

(b. 1893)

ARTHUR BENJAMIN IS an Australian composer. In 1950 he was invited by the Australian Broadcasting Commission to re-visit his country of birth, where he had not been for twenty-two years. His trip was partly to celebrate the fiftieth anniversary of his first public appearance there as a concert pianist, which, the reader can work out, took place at the age of seven! For this occasion he had specially written a new Piano Concerto for himself to play: the solo part is big, almost Lisztian. The composer describes the work as 'a descendant of the rhetorical concerto of the nineteenth century—a pianist's work!' The world first performance, with Eugene Goossens conducting, took place at Sydney (where Benjamin was born) and was an enormous success; he gave no less than seven subsequent performances of the work in Australia during the next two weeks. In England the first performance took place at the 1952 Cheltenham Festival where once again the enormous fluency and effectiveness of the solo part was noted.

Arthur Benjamin, you will have gathered, more or less started life as a pianist: as he put it,[1] 'One of my early memories of the old Queensland days is crawling beneath the piano to hear my mother play. By the time I was three I was something of a pianist myself.' As a youth of seventeen he came to England to study at the Royal College of Music. Life was pleasant in those days: the student lived carefully but comfortably, with enough money to go to concerts and to visit occasionally the Café Royal, then in its heyday

[1] In his not yet completed autobiography: most entertaining extracts from it were printed in *Music and Letters* of July, 1950.

as a rendezvous of figures famous in London's artistic history. And what a distinguished students' orchestra the Royal College had in those days, with players like Leon Goossens, Ernest Hall, Aubrey Brain, and as leader none other than Eugene Goossens. At the College, Benjamin took piano lessons from an uncle, Frederic Cliffe, and learnt something of general musicianship under Thomas Dunhill. Several reference books, including the Supplementary Volume of Grove, state that Benjamin's first published work was a String Quartet, of 1924. This seems to be inaccurate, for in 1911, Dunhill, who acted as adviser to a firm of publishers, asked Arthur Benjamin to write two piano pieces for children. These were duly written, sold outright for two guineas, and published. In the following year he won—he still does not quite know how—one of the two open scholarships for composition awarded that year at the Royal College; the other, by the way, went to a young man with whom he was already friendly and has remained so ever since—Herbert Howells. So Benjamin went to Stanford for composition and Sir Frederick Bridge for fugue.

Throughout the 1914-18 war he saw active service in France, both in the Infantry and the Flying Corps. Soon after demobilisation he returned to Sydney to become for two or three years Professor of piano at the Conservatorium. But of his twin interests, piano and composition, the latter was winning the day, and could obviously be exercised with greater scope in London. So here he settled in the early 1920's, and he stayed for some fifteen years, with interspersed examining and adjudicating tours for the Associated Board. Though his main interest had by now become firmly fixed on composition, he accepted a Professorship of piano at the Royal College of Music, and among many pupils of his who are now outstanding in the musical world was Benjamin Britten. The second world war found him in Canada, teaching piano at Vancouver, and conducting the Symphony Orchestra there for the Canadian Broadcasting Corporation. He remained in Canada until 1946.

Thus Arthur Benjamin's musical career, so far, has been

worked out in three continents. Now the wanderer seems to have settled happily in an attractive mews-flat near Regent's Park, very close to where the late Constant Lambert lived, and within sound, if not sight, of the Zoo. Incidentally, one of the earliest performances of Constant Lambert's *Rio Grande* that I remember was given at a house-warming party of Arthur Benjamin's well before the war: Benjamin played the piano, Constant Lambert juggled with the vast array of percussion instruments, Walton turned over and Hubert Foss conducted.

Arthur Benjamin impresses one as a buoyant and ceaselessly active person: he admits that he cannot just rest, even on holiday. In 1949 for example, when he was taking a vacation in Italy, he wrote a good deal of the autobiography to which I have alluded above. Again on the sea trip back from Australia, apart from being able to go swimming each day in the pool on board ship (his favourite recreations are swimming and cooking), he found time to work, among other things, on a new *Divertimento for Oboe and Strings*, based on little-known music of Gluck. If this turns out to be as effective and grateful as Benjamin's previous Oboe Concerto, based on music of Cimarosa (recorded by Leon Goossens), it will be an excellent addition to the oboe repertoire.

Last year when he was completing the score of his opera *The Tale of Two Cities*, commissioned by the Arts Council under the Festival of Britain Competition, I had occasion to visit him: the first object that caught my eye in his room was a capacious, sloped architect's desk—what a sensible thing for a composer to acquire—with 32-stave paper specially made in Australia to accommodate the decidedly full scoring of this opera. Benjamin has previously written smaller-scale pieces for the stage—*Prima Donna*, for example, which waited fifteen years for a performance, and was an enormous success in 1949, when the London Opera Club produced it: it contains at least one 'smash hit'—or whatever is the equivalent phrase used in dignified musical circles—a 'Drinking Song' for the three male characters. *The Tale of Two Cities* (from Dickens's novel) is, on the other hand, an opera in the

grand romantic manner, 'a 32-stave sort of work' as Arthur
Benjamin described it. Curiously enough, the libretti of both
Prima Donna and *The Tale of Two Cities* are by Cedric
Cliffe, son of Benjamin's first piano professor in England,
mentioned above.

A propos 'smash hits', undoubtedly Benjamin's best-
known piece of music, heard on every conceivable combination of instruments,[1] is his *Jamaican Rumba*. Benjamin is by
no means displeased that this one short piece of immensely
captivating light music brings him in year after year a sub-
stantial proportion of his income. And, just as Somerset
Maugham once admitted his delight that he was a *financially
successful* playwright, so also Benjamin told me with satisfaction that he can now live purely on his income from composition. Though he has in the past done some exceptionally good
film scores (among them *The Master of Bankdam*, the
instructional piece *Steps of the Ballet*, *The Scarlet Pimper-
nel*, and a splendid early Hitchcock picture, *The Man Who
Knew Too Much*) he does not therefore have to continue to
do films in order to live.

It is natural that, with his expert knowledge and understanding of piano playing, Benjamin should enjoy writing for
the piano. In addition to the Concerto I have mentioned, there
are a number of solo works of varying grades of difficulty,
the easier ones just as skilful and attractive as the more
difficult ones. Among educational albums is that entitled
Brumas Tunes (influenced by Benjamin's living near the
Zoo? 'Brumas' was a baby polar bear which received considerable attention from the public a year or two ago but
now, like many a juvenile star, has faded): these are five
pieces of about lower grade with such titles as 'Brumas
learns to swim', 'Brumas sleeps', and so on, and with entertaining illustrations. Slightly more difficult is the album *Let's
go Hiking*. Here are five short pieces, among them 'We set
out', a brisk piece in common time with some useful left-hand
work; 'The Quiet Countryside' and 'A Rest by the Brooklet'.

[1] Among other recordings there is that by Rawicz and Landauer
here, and versions by both Heifetz and William Primrose in America.

both tranquil pieces, affording good exercise in legato playing; and a noisy, knockabout affair, descriptive of the steam roundabout at a village fair. A degree more difficult still are two books of *Fantasies*. These were written for a very specific purpose, which is best described by the composer's own prefatory words:

During the last ten years of examining for the Associated Board of the Royal Schools of Music, London, I find the technical side of pianoforte playing showing a steady and marked improvement, but the expressive-musical side does not show a similar advancement. With this in mind I have written these little *Fantasies* in the hope that tone-quality and tone-gradation, phrasing, rhythm and (last but not least) pedalling will all be given due consideration. In short, they are studies more for artistic playing than for technical agility. I think you will find that they sound much more difficult than they actually are!

In the category of concert piano solos, really difficult, I recommend his *Scherzino* and *Siciliana*, the former calling specially for expert light staccato playing; and the *Pastorale, Arioso and Finale*.

Benjamin has written relatively little for voices (apart from operas), but a group of two-part songs needs to be mentioned here, in particular the setting of 'A Tall Story'. This is the greatest fun which any choir of young singers would enjoy: it is not elementary but is so entertaining that the choir will make light of the occasional tricky bits; a deft pianist is needed. The words, author unknown, are the old bosun's story:

> *"Tis a hundred years', said the bosun bold,*
> *'Since I was a boy at sea;*
> *'Tis a hundred years, so I've been told,*
> *And that's the truth,' said he.*
> *'We sailed one day from Milford Bay,*
> *The North Pole for to see;*
> *And we found it too, without much ado,*
> *And that's the truth', said he.* etc.

Benjamin has provided most witty music with an extremely

happy idea at the recurring line: ' "And that's the truth", said he.'

Wit is present, too, in some of Benjamin's orchestral music, for example the *Light Music Suite* and the sparkling *Overture to an Italian Comedy,* recorded in America by the Chicago Symphony Orchestra under F. Stock: this is in fact a concert version of the overture to *Prima Donna.* But it would be a mistake to overlook his more serious and ambitious works, the biggest being his Symphony No. 1. This is a rich and dramatic composition, written in Vancouver, and first heard here at the Cheltenham Festival of 1949, with Barbirolli conducting. The *Ballade for Strings* is a concert work of depth and unaffected lyricism. A fairly early work (1932) is the Violin Concerto: on re-reading it lately—it is regrettable that opportunities of re-hearing it are so rare—I found it full of excellent stuff.

There is not a great deal of chamber music. But for his friend William Primrose he wrote a Sonata for Viola and Piano, the three movements being sub-titled Elegy, Waltz, and Toccata. This work is also available for viola and orchestra, though in my view it is less happy in orchestral form. A Sonatina for Cello and Piano has the merit of being very playable, with a particularly charming Minuet as its middle movement.

There is room in British music today for a composer of Arthur Benjamin's qualities; his music has a warmth and attractiveness which are none too common, while its idiom is of our time but in no way extreme. There is much to admire, too, in a composer who, as I hope I have made clear, will take just as much trouble and delight in writing a little part-song or piece of teaching piano music as in writing . . . well, shall we say, works employing 32-stave scoring paper!

VI

E. J. MOERAN

(1894 - 1950)

ERNEST JOHN MOERAN met his death on December 1st, 1950, a few weeks before his fifty-sixth birthday. The tragic circumstances are recalled briefly here because they have some relevance to an appreciation of his music. For some time Moeran had been living, not in England, but in what has been called his second home, County Kerry, in the extreme south-western corner of Ireland. He was out walking, as was his habit, in a strong Atlantic gale, and watching the effect of the storm on the sea of Kenmare Bay. He suddenly fell from a pier, due to a heart attack, and the roughness of the sea prevented rescuers in a boat from reaching him in time. Natural surroundings, and particularly the violently changing moods of this part of the Atlantic coast, had a great influence in originating and shaping Moeran's music. He once said that the slow movement of his Symphony, completed in this same County Kerry twelve years earlier, was 'sea music'. I do not think it is too fanciful or melodramatic to suggest, therefore, that he met his death in seeking and storing inspiration for further works reflecting the mood of this Irish environment.

Moeran's father was Irish, a minister from the adjoining County Cork, and so is his widow, the 'cellist Peers Coetmore. But Moeran himself was born near London and lived in England a good deal of his life, especially in Norfolk. Here the flat sand dunes and marshes provide the second strong topographical influence on his music. In this part of England, too, arose his abiding interest in the folk songs of the countryside, those sometimes touching and sometimes robust tunes which are so rapidly disappearing under conditions of modern industrialised life. Many of these tunes he collected and arranged, and a few are mentioned below. Furthermore the thematic element in his own original music often derives from folk song, though he rarely uses actual folk songs. In that his music reflects the influence both of natural surroundings and of the traditional folk-music handed down from generation to generation in those surroundings, Moeran followed the footsteps of R. Vaughan Williams, a close personal friend of his. It is to Vaughan Williams, incidentally, that Moeran dedicated his *Lonely Waters,* a piece for small orchestra based on a fragment of song 'still frequently to be heard on Saturday nights at certain inns in the broads district of East Norfolk'—thus Moeran wrote.

Moeran's output was not particularly big: he was a discriminating worker and discarded many of his earlier compositions. It is significant that his Symphony, already mentioned, was not written until he was in his middle forties—first symphonies usually appear much earlier in a composer's career—and in this case the suggestion that he should write a symphony had come to him more than ten years earlier, from the Irish conductor, Sir Hamilton Harty. Since the Symphony he wrote rather more frequently for orchestra, his works including a Cello Concerto, written as a wedding present for his wife; a Sinfonietta, a most firm and lively work; a light Serenade, an ideal Prom work (it was first heard at the Promenade Concerts in 1948); and a Violin Concerto —all these orchestral works were written either during the last war or immediately after it.

At the time of his death Moeran was said to be working on a second symphony. I feel, however, that he was not, in essence, a symphonic composer, though he could invent good, strong themes (the openings of both the Symphony and the Violin Concerto show this): the handling and development of such themes and the large structure implied in symphonic thinking sometimes failed to receive assured treatment at his hands. Perhaps Moeran was more of an intuitive than an intellectual composer: he was happier working in smaller forms—especially songs and short choral pieces, chamber music of an unpretentious nature (the String Quartet and the String Trio are good examples), and piano pieces. Thus, except for the fact that his piano music represents a rather less important part of it, Moeran's output resembles that of John Ireland, with whom he studied composition at the Royal College of Music after the 1914-18 war. There is some similarity, too, in their actual type of writing. Both are lyrical composers, poetical and imaginative, their melodic lines often clothed in luxuriant chromatic harmonies. Neither composer's works show the slightest evidence of the linear, sometimes angular contrapuntal writing once fashionable in twentieth-century music. Indeed, in Moeran's case one wishes at times that there were a bit more contrapuntal interest, for his harmonic usage, stemming from that of Delius, cloys occasionally; particularly his reliance on chord-sequences built on a bass descending by semitones.

Of his fifteen or so piano pieces, several are difficult and only one can be called easy. This is an attractive, straightforward two-page piece, based, I believe, on an Irish tune, entitled *The White Mountain*. On its second appearance, the tune is given to the left hand, marked 'well to the fore', and providing good practice for *cantabile* playing. More characteristic, and not very much more difficult, are the *Two Pieces* (Prelude and Berceuse): the former is an especially alluring miniature, with its echo—unintentional?—of 'Tom, Tom, the Piper's Son'; it needs *legato* playing in both hands, without too much reliance on the sustaining pedal. A much earlier piece (1922) of only moderate difficulty is *On a May Morning*: it is none the worse for showing a distinct influence, understandable at that date, of John Ireland. Of the *Two Legends* of a year or two later, *A Folk Story* is perhaps the more grateful to play and is an effectively evocative piece, entailing a fair left-hand stretch and a right hand able to execute light arabesque passages at reasonable speed.

All the foregoing are, as can be guessed from their titles, rather delicate, expressive pieces. But Moeran had his robust, vigorous side, too, shown excellently in one of the better-known of his more difficult piano solos—*Bank Holiday*. This has caught the carefree mood appropriate to its title and has a Percy Grainger-ish bounce to it: the nimble pianist will enjoy it and the amateur need not be daunted by it, even if he has to take the speed at something less than the prescribed 'crotchet = 168'. Similarly the player may have to think twice (and practise a great deal) before he tackles at 'dotted minim = 92–96' the last, and I think the best, of a set of three early piano pieces, *At the Horse Fair*, in syncopated three-four time and fun to play (a good recital piece, too, which one never seems to come across in programmes). *Windmills*, from a set of three Fancies also dating from the early 1920s, is occasionally heard and is a fine study in rapid *piano* playing, *sempre legato*. Among the really advanced and more elaborate pieces, *Stalham River* is possibly the most notable.

For choirs Moeran catered well, if not as prolifically as one would have wished. Many schools and unison choirs will have enjoyed his setting of *The Jolly Carter*, a gay folk-song from Suffolk which Moeran himself collected. This was originally published, in 1925, as a unison song; the year before his death he re-arranged it admirably for mixed voices, for T. B. Lawrence and his well-known Fleet Street Choir. At the same time Moeran also arranged for this group a folk-song from Norfolk, *The Sailor and Young Nancy*. Other unison songs include an original setting of *Christmas Day in the Morning* ('As I sat under a sycamore tree')—it needs a good pianist, by the way; *Commendation of Music*, a spacious tune, apt for massed singing; and a distinctive and haunting setting of the over-frequently-set, *Come Away, Death*. Shakespeare also provided the words for two useful part-songs: *When Icicles Hang by the Wall*, and *The Lover and His Lass*, this latter being quite one of the most captivating modern treatments of these words.

In 1933 and 1939 respectively appeared two important sequences of part-songs for S.A.T.B. unaccompanied, *Songs of Springtime* and *Phyllida and Corydon*. The former is one of his best works and, not being excessively difficult, can be warmly recommended to any mixed choir of enterprise. It comprises settings of seven Elizabethan poems, two being Shakespearian ('Under the Greenwood Tree', and 'Sigh no more, ladies', that piece of advice being pronounced mainly in five-eight time!). The other poems in this set, include the well-known 'Spring, the sweet Spring', by Nashe, Herrick's 'To Daffodils', and a Drinking Song by William Browne which will be new to many people, a rousing affair, ending: 'To drink of the sherry, That makes us so merry, And plump as the lusty grape'. The other, later, choral suite *Phyllida and Corydon*, dedicated to Constant Lambert, is more difficult, and the freshness and charm of the earlier set seem to be less in evidence.

As a man, Moeran was companionable yet shy, to the point of being occasionally brusque in speech. When one broke down the reserve, one could never fail to be impressed by the complete honesty of his conversation and of his downright opinions. He disliked any suspicion of cant or of superficial smartness, whether in people or art. Among his friends were distinguished musicians such as Constant Lambert and Patrick Hadley, the Cambridge Professor of Music, also an East Anglian composer, by the way; Moeran was very much at home in the company of orchestral players, perhaps his very closest friend being Pat Ryan, first clarinettist of the Hallé Orchestra. I last saw Moeran when that orchestra was playing at the annual summer Festival of British Contemporary Music at Cheltenham (where he was living for a time). I mentioned to him that my hotel boasted a croquet lawn, and he, being devoted to this game, came round to play on several occasions. I have a vivid and touching memory of his explaining, gravely and courteously, some of the finer points of croquet to a group of children assembled on that lawn.

Moeran was a keen follower of all kinds of contemporary music and was generous in his appreciation of other people's work, even when he was not entirely in sympathy with it. He himself was not an adventurer but his music has warmth and honesty, qualities that count for more than an artificial striving after novelty. He was probably the most gifted of the

group of English composers who succeeded Vaughan
Williams, Ireland and Bax, and preceded the younger school
of Walton and Britten. His tragic and untimely death was
a real loss to this country's music.

VII

GORDON JACOB

(b. 1895)

I T S E E M S T O be an accepted custom in this country to
refer to any composer under the age of sixty as a younger
composer, and at precisely his sixtieth birthday to promote
him, overnight as it were, to the status of a senior, veteran
composer, and before you know where you are, to a 'Grand
Old Man' of English music. Perhaps in the case of Dr Gordon
Jacob I may compromise in this tricky business of classifica-
tion and call him one of the younger of our senior composers. He was born in Upper Norwood, within stone-throw-
ing distance of that much lamented edifice, the Crystal Palace.
(There are other composers, by the way, who could in their
young days similarly have hurled stones at the Crystal Palace,
namely Coleridge-Taylor, William Hurlstone and Joseph
Holbrooke: but, as readers will know, composers are not
addicted to this aggressive habit.) Gordon Jacob was educated at Dulwich College, still therefore within sight of the
Palace of Glass, and immediately after the 1914-18 war, went
to the Royal College of Music. He is of the same generation
as many other distinguished R.C.M.-trained British composers, including Herbert Howells, E. J. Moeran, Eugene
Goossens and Patrick Hadley. Jacob studied composition
there under Stanford and Charles Wood, and conducting
under Boult. But, quite aside from what he learned at the
Royal College of Music, he had had during the 1914-18 war
the best possible practical experience in orchestration. He
was imprisoned in Germany for some twenty months, and in
the prison camp he organised and conducted a small band
of players—flute, clarinet, cornet, violins, cellos and piano—
and, as well as conducting these fellow-prisoners, he himself

necessarily had to arrange all the music for this particular, rather specialised group of enthusiasts.

Gordon Jacob has continued since his student days to be closely associated with the Royal College of Music, and has for some twenty-five years been a professor there. (He has also taught at Birkbeck and Morley Colleges, and has acted as examiner for the Associated Board.) Today, in order to spend the maximum amount of his time in actual composition, he limits his teaching at the Royal College to one day per week. The rest of his time he spends at his quiet home in the New Forest. Previously he lived for many years in Surrey not far from Vaughan Williams, and there are links between the two composers, apart from their both having been students at the Royal College of Music, and professors there. One of Gordon Jacob's orchestral works is a Chaconne based upon a theme of Vaughan Williams: the theme is, in fact, that serene, broad tune, the 'Saraband of the Sons of God', from *Job*. Then, in a recently published book,[1] Vaughan Williams himself has paid a remarkable tribute to the younger composer, in these terms:

He was, at one time, nominally my pupil, though there was nothing I could teach him, at all events in the matter of technique, which he did not know better than I. Since then I have often asked his advice on points of orchestration, as indeed I would gladly do in any branch of the composer's art.

To meet Gordon Jacob suggests immediately the deliberate, honest and straightforward craftsman. There is nothing pretentious about his manner, and though he exhibits occasionally a shrewd wit, his conversation is homely rather than flashingly—or, as so often, flashily—brilliant. One feels he ought to be comfortably smoking a pipe—and so he usually is. He is interested in teaching, though he recognises that to 'teach' composition is rather to misuse the word 'teach': one can merely guide and encourage. Or discourage: Gordon Jacob agreed with me that it was rather depressing to find today such a formidable number of people writing down

[1] *R. Vaughan Williams*: by Hubert J. Foss, published by Harrap.

music on paper, the bulk of it not actually bad, but not positively good. However, as he put it, one needs 90 per cent manure to enable 10 per cent of the real product to flourish. One thing he is insistent upon in his teaching, namely, that it is ideas that matter and not the idiom in which they happen to be expressed. And, as a rider to this, he pointed out that if it suits a composer to express his ideas in a fairly traditional idiom, his technique must be on an even higher level than if his idiom were more advanced. Thus in a sense it is easier, technically, to write so-called progressive music than to make a more traditional and accepted style interesting and fresh.

This is pertinent to Gordon Jacob's own music which, while not being the least bit archaic, is firmly founded on traditional methods. It is melodious, harmonically clean, and in faster movements it has strong and clear-cut rhythms, often with some syncopation. It is thoroughly likable music, and invariably it 'comes off' well, without being superficial or exhibitionistic in the sense that it parades its technical adroitness. In his book, *Orchestral Technique*,[1] he pertinently remarks: 'The object of orchestration is not to show how clever one is—that is of no interest to anyone—but to present the music in its clearest and most appropriate orchestral form.' But it is certainly true that in the use of the orchestra—and the bulk of his music is orchestral—there is no more adroit person in this country, and I doubt whether there are many as adroit in Europe.

Above all, Jacob believes in being practical. In the same book, on the first page, he makes the following remarks, and every music student would do well to carry these few pithy sentences always in the forefront of his mind:

Do not imagine that attention to practical detail argues a defective artistic sense. Leave such ideas to romantically-minded novelists. To musicians music is not only an art. It is also a craft, and a complex and difficult one.

Because of his own practising of what he preaches—an unswerving attention to practical detail—his music never

[1] Oxford University Press.

D

makes excessive demands upon the players: and if he has the task of writing deliberately easy music, he can do so without in any way diminishing the interest and the purely musical values of the work in question. A good example of this is the *Denbigh Suite* for String Orchestra, written for Howell's School, Denbigh, a most attractive affair, with some pleasant cross-rhythms in its Praeludium. Also of no great difficulty are the *Fantasia on the Alleluia Hymn* for Orchestra, and the *Suite in F* for Small Orchestra. Both these are indeed pieces which one customarily hears in the programmes of professional orchestras, but there is no intrinsic reason why either of them should not be tackled by the more enterprising amateur orchestra or public school orchestra. Such organisations would undoubtedly enjoy playing, from the latter work, the brisk Overture and the March which concludes the Suite.

Throughout his composing career, Gordon Jacob has shown a particular interest in wind instruments, their clear and distinct timbres evidently having an attraction for him. In the chamber-music field he has written, for example, a Clarinet Quintet, an Oboe Quartet and a Serenade for Eight Woodwind Instruments, which was done at the Cambridge Festival in 1950. Then there are various works for solo wind instrument and orchestra, the Oboe Concerto and the Rhapsody for Cor Anglais, for instance, and, most notable and likeable of all, the Concerto for Bassoon, Strings and Percussion, written for the very distinguished player Archie Camden. This is not merely a welcome addition to an almost non-existent repertoire, but is undoubtedly one of his finest works. May I suggest that if the gramophone recording companies in this country wanted to turn their attention to Gordon Jacob's music—it is rather astonishing that they have not so far done so—they could do no better than record this Bassoon Concerto.

Two other orchestral works should be mentioned here: one is the Suite No. 3 (1949) specially written to celebrate the seventy-fifth anniversary of the Bournemouth Municipal Orchestra, which is so creditably associated with performance of new British music. The other work is the *Passacaglia on a Well-known Theme,* the well-known theme being in fact 'Oranges and Lemons'. This is a most attractive and exciting piece, which captures the attention right from its opening bars—the tune is heard on solo horn and solo harp alone—to its riotous end. This is far from being an academic piece, but the perceptive listener will not fail to hear the augmentation of the theme thundered out in the bass, during the closing pages.

I have already mentioned that the bulk of Jacob's music is for orchestra. But he is equally at home in writing for choirs. A fairly early work, a Cantata for Children, entitled *The Birthday,* was written for the Reigate and Redhill and District Musical Competition Festival, and consists of ten songs for unison or two-part singing. A recent work, even more interesting, is entitled *A Goodly Heritage,* and was commissioned by the Women's Choirs of Surrey for performance during the Festival of Britain period, with accompaniment of Strings. These choirs would, I am sure, agree that they have here got a first-class work. There are twelve songs, each reflecting some aspect of the countryside, for two- and three-part chorus. The words are from various sources, including Shakespeare's 'Under the Greenwood Tree' and 'When Icicles Hang by the Wall', Shelley's 'Evening', a three-part setting of John Bunyan's 'The Cuckoo', and an entertaining setting of an anonymous poem entitled 'The Rewards of Farming' (with a certain amount of nostalgia I quote a few lines: 'I eat my own Lamb, My Chickens and Ham, I shear my own Fleece and I wear it'). And the work ends with a three-part setting of William Cornish's 'Pleasure it is'.

This Cantata is not the only work which Gordon Jacob prepared for the period of the 1951 Festival of Britain: there were two other important pieces, both showing, as it happens, his partiality for wind instruments. First of all, a Concerto for Horn and String Orchestra, written for the incomparable Mr Dennis Brain. The other work, a commission from the Arts Council, was written for a large-scale military band, or bands, with Kneller Hall in mind, and is laid out as a series of eleven movements. These are alternately for a smaller group of trumpets and trombones, and for a full military band. The two contingents are used antiphonally and come together only in the Finale.

Gordon Jacob is perhaps at his best on festive occasions: may there be many more such which will give us opportunity to hear again this splendid occasional piece—desirably with large forces and out-of-doors!

VIII

EDMUND RUBBRA

(b. 1901)

EDMUND RUBBRA WAS born in Northampton in 1901.
While most of his colleagues and contemporaries among
native composers have had a not too uncomfortable upbringing, that cannot be said of Rubbra. Early on he was
brought into contact with the harsher aspects of life. His
father was employed in a boot factory, and he himself as a
schoolboy supplemented his family's meagre income by run-
ning errands after hours. He left school at the age of four-
teen and worked for some years as a railway clerk: unpic-
turesque indeed! Such spare time as was at his disposal he
devoted entirely to music, studying contemporary work with
particular enthusiasm. In those days, up to the age of about
nineteen, he was helped by Cyril Scott, though he did not
study intensively with him. A scholarship to Reading University enabled him to work under Gustav Holst, and it is
especially to him and to R. O. Morris, with whom he later
studied counterpoint at the Royal College of Music, that he
acknowledges an enormous debt. He also worked for a time
under Vaughan Williams, whose influence in his subsequent
music can be traced. As well as studying composition, he took
piano lessons, and, as listeners to the radio know, he is an
outstandingly good chamber-pianist.

He lived in London for some time between the two wars,
married in 1933 the French violinist Antoinette Chaplin, for
whom he wrote his Second Violin Sonata, which was his first
work to be recorded. In 1934 he moved out of London to a
simple cottage near Aylesbury, and has happily lived there
since that date.

If his only activity were composing he could, and I believe

would, never leave the quiet country home that he has made for himself. But his life is a busy and varied one. In 1947 he was appointed as Lecturer in Music at Oxford University, giving two lectures a week, one of them on counterpoint. Also he takes part in many concerts, broadcast and otherwise, with the Piano Trio which he formed during the 1939–1945 war, and to which I shall refer later: and it is perhaps not generally known that he writes regularly most admirable reviews of music and gramophone records in various magazines.

It was in the course of his war service with the Royal Artillery that he was seconded to give chamber music concerts, and met as associate William Pleeth, the well-known young cellist. For him Rubbra was later to write his *Soliloquy* for solo cello and chamber orchestra, a work that is too rarely heard, and the Cello and Piano Sonata. With Pleeth, too, he formed the Piano Trio now known as the Rubbra-Gruenberg-Pleeth Trio.

Rubbra's output is considerable: his latest work, a Viola Concerto which was first performed in April, 1953, is his Opus 75. He has written music in most forms except opera: even that statement needs qualification, since, when I once commented to him that he was one of the few native composers who had not written an opera or was not engaged now in writing one, he told me that he did, in fact, in 1934 write an opera based on an Arabian Nights story. But it has never been performed. A more surprising thing is that, though, as I have said, Rubbra is a splendid pianist, he has written very little indeed for the piano—apart from using it in various chamber works. Quite recently, however, he did compose for Cyril Scott's 70th birthday a Prelude and Fugue on a theme taken from the slow movement of Cyril Scott's First Piano Sonata. It is an interestingly constructed piece which can be tackled by any player who is up to the standard of, say, the moderately difficult pieces in Bach's *Forty-Eight*. This piece itself is somewhat Bachian, and throughout a good deal of his work there is some influence of Bach's music to be felt. Quite early in his career, in 1929, an article on Rubbra stated that 'he has always been able to think more clearly in a contrapuntal medium than in a vertical harmonic one, and he holds that the way out of our present-day harmonic *cul-de-sac* is by means of a vivid new contrapuntal technique'. He has not changed his ideas basically since then, though his technique has broadened and he has perhaps found a more satisfactorily working compromise between the vertical and the horizontal.

Apart from some easy teaching pieces for piano which Rubbra contributed in 1952 to a series of graded piano albums by various composers, the only other work to be mentioned in which the piano is used as a solo instrument is the *Sinfonia Concertante* for piano and orchestra. This work was written in 1936, and revised some seven years later. It consists of three movements, Fantasia, Saltarello, and a final Prelude and Fugue written in memory of Gustav Holst. This last movement is in some ways the most interesting of the three, its serene end being especially notable.

Undoubtedly his outstanding achievement in the orchestral category is his series of five symphonies, of which probably Nos. 3 and 5 are the best known. The latter has been recorded under British Council auspices, conducted by Barbirolli. Many listeners will also remember for a long time the most revealing performance of this work given by Stokowski during a visit of his to Great Britain. The most immediately attractive of its three movements is the middle one, based on a catchy tune which resembles in type a French folk dance. It is played alone by first horn at the opening. The other movements have a breadth and spaciousness, and above all a sense of growth and direction, which are among Rubbra's strongest characteristics. These qualities are equally in evidence in the four-movement Third Symphony, the last movement being a set of seven variations and a fugue upon a slowish 3/2 theme: it may be noted in passing that 3/2 and 6/4 are time signatures commonly to be met in Rubbra's works, but rare, surely, in many contemporary composers' music.

Among his chamber music, apart from the works already

mentioned, are two string quartets, the second of which has been recorded by the Griller String Quartet; and on humbler lines, an Air and Variations for pipes, and a set of Meditations on *Cœurs Desolés*—a medieval chanson—for recorder (or flute or oboe) and harpsichord (or piano.) Both parts are quite playable.

The generally broad lines of Rubbra's style fit him naturally for writing for choirs, and among his outstanding choral settings is the motet entitled *The Morning Watch,* the words by the seventeenth-century poet Henry Vaughan. This was commissioned by the Musicians' Benevolent Fund and performed at the first St. Cecilia's Day Festival at the Royal Albert Hall, London, in 1946. (Rubbra's original plan of making this setting part of a choral symphony did not materialise.) It is for the most part in slow or moderate tempo, though with occasional more animated sections. But the most impressive parts of the work are probably its dignified opening and the final section (again note the 3/2 time signature) at the words

> *So in my bed*
> *That curtained grave, though sleep, like ashes, hide*
> *My lamp, and life, both shall in thee abide.*

These words are set in unison for the whole choir against a gently moving counterpoint in the orchestra, which carries on alone in a short and simple epilogue.

Two other notable commissioned works are, firstly, Rubbra's contribution to the collection of *a capella* pieces, *A Garland for the Queen,* written to commemorate Queen Elizabeth II's Coronation in 1953—his setting of Christopher Hassall's *Salutation* is the final one in this anthology and in many ways the most impressive. The other work, commissioned for the Festival of Britain 1951, is Rubbra's *Festival Te Deum* for soprano, chorus and orchestra, a setting of great brilliance, making quite considerable demands on the chorus. Mention must be made, too, of Rubbra's Liturgical Settings, *The Canterbury Mass,* and the *Latin Mass* for unaccompanied chorus.

Of all composers discussed in this book, Rubbra is the plainest.[1] Sibelius's often quoted remark about his own music —to the effect that, while other modern composers were busy fabricating highly coloured cocktails, he offered the public just a straight glass of pure cold water—could with reservation be applied to Rubbra, though I am not suggesting that there is a stylistic resemblance between the two: if one wanted to point to a foreign composer who affords some parallels with Rubbra, it would be rather to Bruckner than Sibelius. But the fact is that, without the aid of superficial attractions, Rubbra's music can give most intense satisfaction: the audience which finds that satisfaction is at present, admittedly, a fairly small section of the musical public. But his work possesses such inner strength and integrity that it may well outlast the music of many of his contemporaries which is today more widely, but less intensely, appreciated.

[1] His new Viola Concerto, however, shows a more extroverted spirit, a greater brilliance and outward appeal than have so far been customary in Rubbra's music.

IX

SIR WILLIAM WALTON

(b. 1902)

SIR WILLIAM WALTON, a truly international figure, has done at least as much as any other living English composer to demonstrate that our native music is today no longer the parochial, hole-in-the-corner affair it was previously judged to be, but is a vital art worthy of appreciation by world standards. Few musicians of any nationality, indeed, would deny that Walton is already to be classed in the highest rank of European composers of the twentieth century. It is not without significance that the two most distinguished violinists of America, and probably of the world—Heifetz and Menuhin—each commissioned a work from Walton. Heifetz gave the first performance of the Violin Concerto in Cleveland, Ohio, in 1939: Menuhin played the Violin and Piano Sonata for the first time at Drury Lane Theatre in 1950, the piano part being played by Louis Kentner, who is, by the way, Menuhin's brother-in-law.

Walton has achieved this high international status with singularly few works, and it is difficult to think of any comparable case in modern musical history where smallness of output goes with such tremendous reputation. Possibly Manuel de Falla provides some parallel. Walton's first real success occurred as long as thirty years ago. This was the immensely popular, amusing, skilful and charming *Façade Entertainment* for reciting voice and seven instruments, with poems of Edith Sitwell. In the intervening years Walton has composed six major works, a handful of smaller ones and some very distinguished film music. But the matter and quality of these few works has amply compensated for the relatively small quantity. He has written one symphony only, but it is regarded by many people as the finest English symphony of this century. Of the two concertos for a stringed instrument and orchestra, both are outstanding in the modern repertoire, and certainly the Viola Concerto can be claimed as perhaps the most distinguished work by any living composer for that still rather neglected instrument. Of his two choral works, *Belshazzar's Feast* was a landmark in modern English choral music and never fails to provide an overwhelming experience for performers and audience alike whenever it is done today—and it is done surprisingly often, considering its difficulties. Similarly, when his String Quartet appeared in 1947—it was his first mature chamber music composition—it turned out to be one of the very best of twentieth-century English quartets.

It is known that Walton has been working for some time on an opera which, since it was commissioned by the BBC (to whom all praise), it is as well to make clear is to be an opera for the opera house and not for the studio. The story is based on Chaucer's *Troilus and Cressida,* and the librettist is Christopher Hassall (who incidentally is that boon to composers, rare since Boito, a poet who is also a trained musician —he studied with Dr W. H. Harris at Oxford). When the opera is completed—at the time of writing, Walton is working on the last act—one has the firm feeling that it will again prove to be a completely outstanding example in its category.

Since his earliest days Walton has been, as I have implied above, a great ambassador for British music abroad: many of his works have been first heard out of this country, or have been first played by non-English artists, such as the two violinists already referred to. His gay *Portsmouth Point* Overture was first heard in 1926 at Zürich, at the International Festival of Contemporary Music. When, three years later, the Viola Concerto received its première, the soloist was none other than Paul Hindemith. The Overture *Scapino* was written specially for the fiftieth anniversary of the foundation of the Chicago Symphony Orchestra, and dedicated to its conductor, Frederick Stock. He first performed it in 1941.

When this Overture was revised nearly ten years later, the conductor who first gave the revised version was Furtwängler.

Italy is a country to which Walton has always been attracted, having lived and visited there on many occasions: much of his opera was written in Ischia, a small island off the west coast. One of his earliest visits to Italy was in 1928, when the *Façade Entertainment* was given at the International Festival at Siena. The speaker on that occasion, as on many subsequent occasions, was the late Mr Constant Lambert, who was without his peer in this role. If Edith Sitwell's poems have in their time bewildered English audiences, they must have had an even more strange effect on the Italian audience. None the less, the performance went along very well until the piece entitled *Tarantella* started. Then something like a riot arose in the audience and chaos broke out in the theatre. Walton and the performers found this inexplicable until they realised that in this particular piece Walton had parodied Rossini and this was taken by the audience to be a direct insult to the Italian nation. It is said that an Italian paper, reporting next day, named the composer of *Façade* 'Wanton', which one likes to think was a deliberate misprint.

It must be admitted that earlier performances of *Façade*, even in this country, caused a bit of an uproar, and the fireman at the Aeolian Hall, where it was given publicly, was reported in the press as having stated that 'never in twenty years' experience of recitals at that hall had he known anything like it'. When, however, *Façade* was again done at Aeolian Hall many years later, in 1941, according to Sir Osbert Sitwell the same fireman was still there and by now had given his approval to the work!

Apart from the original form of the work for speaker and instruments, Walton arranged two orchestral suites of the music, which have become immensely popular. Also these are available for piano duet and although they are not especially easy, they are the greatest fun for amateur performers to tackle; the present writer can vouch for this. If one has no partner, certain numbers are also arranged as piano solos, and at least the *Popular Song* and the *Swiss Jodelling Song* can be attempted without fear.

As to original music for piano, Walton has written extremely little: possibly the reason for this is that he is no pianist—Sir Osbert Sitwell has recorded that when he first met Walton and heard him play some of his early compositions, 'he revealed a lack of mastery of the instrument that was altogether unusual'. There is, however, one delightful, if slight, composition of Walton's for piano. This is the collection entitled *Duets for Children*, written for one piano, four hands. Technically the notes and chords and stretches are well within the capabilities of young players. Idiomatically and rhythmically, the pieces are more advanced, and it is just this art of expressing a lively, up-to-date idiom in the easiest possible technical terms that makes the collection so attractive to children (and indeed to grown-up players, who need certainly not be ashamed of looking at this work). The pieces are well varied and include, among the quicker ones, a syncopated *Three-Legged Race*, *Hop Scotch* in five-eight from beginning to end, *Puppets' Dance*, which is in three-four time, but with a good deal of accent *off* the first beat, and a rather Borodin-like *Trumpet Tune* to end with. Then there are expressive short lyrical pieces of great charm such as *The Silent Lake* and *Song at Dusk*. Later the pieces were orchestrated under the title of *Music for Children*, and in this form the work should prove to be as popular a repertoire piece as Bizet's *Jeux d'Enfants*. Later still the pieces were re-arranged for piano solo, in which form they are naturally rather more tricky than in the original duet version, but are not by any means difficult.

The other work of Walton's which can be mentioned in connection with the piano is the *Sinfonia Concertante* for orchestra with piano obbligato. This is an early work, of 1927, but one of great attractiveness and character, particularly in its first movement and the romantic slow movement. The last movement, with its clatter of the 1920s, perhaps does date a bit.

I have referred once or twice above to remarks about

Walton made by his very close friend over a long period of years, Sir Osbert Sitwell. I have drawn these from an absorbingly interesting, as well as entertaining, character sketch of Walton which appears in Volume 4 of Sir Osbert Sitwell's autobiography, *Laughter in the Next Room*.[1] The chapter in question is entitled 'Façade'. I urge the reader to go to this chapter if he wishes to know something about Walton the man. Sir Osbert is particularly revealing when he writes of Walton's early days when he was up at Christ Church, Oxford, having gone there from the Cathedral Choir School. It is said, incidentally, that Walton was, at the age of sixteen, the youngest undergraduate of Oxford University since the time of Henry VIII. At Oxford he received help from Sir Hugh Allen and Dr Henry Ley, but can generally be said to have been self-taught as a composer. When he was seventeen, the young Walton went to live at the Sitwells' house, and there are many diverting stories in this chapter—of his skill in picking a lock when a key was lost, of his extraordinary feat, after six strong men had failed to hoist his piano up the staircase into his room, of doing it singlehanded, apparently 'with a bit of string'. But the reader must go to this chapter himself and I am sure he will enjoy it.

In 1948, Walton paid a visit to South America, on a mission on behalf of the Performing Right Society. There he met the strikingly attractive and lively Argentinian lady who was to become his wife: he married her before returning to this country. Three years later, in 1951, Walton was honoured with a knighthood, receiving this honour, as Elgar had, before reaching the age of fifty. This distinction and the many degrees which have been conferred upon him, he wears easily.

In 1953 he was chosen to compose a new setting for chorus and orchestra for the *Te Deum* for the Coronation of Queen Elizabeth II. The result was a splendid work which formed a musical climax of the service at Westminster Abbey and has already been much performed subsequently in the concert hall.

[1] Published by Macmillan.

William Walton is still a somewhat shy person, as he very noticeably was in his younger days. His conversation is witty, increasingly so in the last few years, and his views on music are acute and sometimes trenchant. He is nothing but a composer. By that I mean that he does not play any instrument, does not teach or lecture (up till a year or two ago he had never even spoken on the radio), and though he is now a first-rate conductor of his own works, he has never, as far as I know, conducted other people's.

Though he can, therefore, devote the bulk of his time to composition, he is a slow and discriminating worker. His language is the language of tradition, with, in several works, some Brahmsian tinge, but his expression is entirely of today. His music has warmth and thematic distinction—he does write real themes and not, as is fashionable today, snippety motives. With these qualities, he can afford to be unprolific: indeed, perhaps it is partly this very lack of fluency in him that gives everything he writes an added intensity and strength.

X

LENNOX BERKELEY

(b. 1903)

IF WE CONSIDER our younger composers, who—if
any—can be described as 'characteristically British' (or,
for that matter, characteristically Italian, or French, or
Spanish) and what do these national labels mean today?
They did mean something in the earlier years of this century,
and did suggest, however roughly, the type of music one
could expect. But nowadays the composer's passport is not
firmly endorsed with his nationality. It may not be entirely
irrelevant to mention that at an International Festival of
Contemporary Music which I attended in Brussels, the most
French-sounding work I heard turned out to have been
written by a Japanese!

Lennox Berkeley is, in any case, a somewhat exceptional
figure in British music. In the first place, his actual nationality is not so clear-cut—he has considerable French blood
in him, both his grandmothers having been of French birth.
Furthermore, for a number of years in the 1920s and 1930s,
at a formative period of his career, he lived and studied in
France. He worked there under the very famous and remarkable teacher, Nadia Boulanger, who has guided an astonishingly high proportion of younger composers in all countries
of the world. Berkeley studied with her, not in order to
acquire a French flavour to his music, but because it was
the natural thing for him to seek in this school of Paris an
appropriate training for developing qualities which were
already latent in him, and a part of his inheritance. Such
qualities as we have been accustomed to associate with Gallic
countries—polish, economy, clarity and graciousness—are
evident, among others, in his music, and since they are

qualities which have been none too common in the twentieth-century renaissance of English composition, they are refreshingly welcome.

But we are jumping ahead: let me first mention a few pertinent biographical facts. Berkeley was born near Oxford in 1903, and was educated at one of the more progressive English public schools, namely Gresham's, Holt. By a coincidence, some ten years later Benjamin Britten was also to be a pupil there: subsequently the two became, and have since remained, the closest of friends. They collaborated together in an orchestral suite based on Spanish folk music (*Mont Juic*), and one of Berkeley's more recent works, the *Stabat Mater,* was not only dedicated to Britten, but was conducted by him at its first performance.

Berkeley returned as an undergraduate to Oxford, where his musical interests were furthered by the help of Dr W. H. Harris, but where he did not pursue music in a wholeheartedly professional way. This stage was not reached until he left Oxford in 1926, and at once went to live in Paris. It was there that I first met him, a good twenty years ago, a more retiring person than he is now. He lived then on the hill of Montmartre, today a rather disappointing tourist quarter, but in the late twenties still maintaining a good deal of its quiet village atmosphere which one can recapture through the paintings of such an artist as Utrillo. He remained in Paris for some seven years, and he acknowledges considerable help in those days from the advice of Ravel. He returned to England, and during the few years prior to 1939 his reputation was already beginning to grow: it made great strides both during the war years and subsequently. It may be mentioned that for a time, in the course of the war, he worked on the programme staff of the B.B.C.: he cannot have been entirely contented at an office, rather than a composer's, desk, but his sojourn at the B.B.C. was certainly not without its point. There he met, also employed there, his future wife. With their two children, they now live in a quiet Regency-period part of London. One would half expect, for reasons which will emerge later, Lennox Berkeley

E

to live by the sea: he has done the next best thing in that his house flanks a canal, on account of which this particular quarter of London is familiarly known as 'Little Venice'.

While the majority of Berkeley's time is spent in composition, he is also a professor at the Royal Academy of Music, and I cannot imagine a more sympathetic one, with his quiet, friendly, and generous understanding.

Especially in recent years, Lennox Berkeley has been steadily writing works in most categories of music, orchestral, piano, chamber music, and works for the solo voice and choirs. He has also done a certain amount of film music, most notably when he was commissioned to write the score for *The First Gentleman*. This was an auspicious, as well as an enjoyable, occasion for Berkeley, since the music was recorded by none other than Sir Thomas Beecham and the Royal Philharmonic Orchestra, and it was the first time, as far as I know, that Sir Thomas worked in a film studio.

I consider that Berkeley's piano music constitutes a most important part of his total output. Not many of our native composers, indeed, have written as much for piano as Berkeley has, or have been so interested in the particular problem of reconciling the contemporary idiom with thoroughly pianistic writing and lay-out. He is himself a good pianist, though not pretending to professional soloist standards: one feels that he takes pleasure in working out ideas and figures in terms of the hands and the keyboard. I can think of no better introduction to his music than the fairly recent set of Six Preludes, recorded (H.M.V.) by the very brilliant young New Zealand pianist, Colin Horsley, for whom also Lennox Berkeley wrote his Piano Concerto. It goes without saying that these Preludes, or some of them, are not easy, but on the other hand at least two of them, numbers four and six, can be tackled with enjoyment by pianists of modest attainments. The fourth has a distinct harmonic flavour of Ravel, the sixth has a tune which sticks in one's mind and which one feels under one's fingers even when away from the keyboard. They are extraordinarily graceful pieces to play. I commend also the fifth for anyone with a nimble mind and reasonably nimble fingers, which together will not be dismayed by the predominant 7/8 rhythm.

Rather easier than this set are the earlier Five Short Pieces, which, like the Six Preludes, contain some examples of the lightly sentimental type of piece which one also associates with the French composer, Francis Poulenc: Berkeley's gifts in this direction seem to be comparable to those of Poulenc at his best, and that surely is high praise.

More difficult works for piano solo include a set of Four Concert Studies and the really difficult Sonata, written a few years ago for Clifford Curzon; this last is an extremely serious work and also contains a good deal of bravura writing, almost Lisztian in its keyboard brilliance.

For two pianos, I must not forget the early Polka, a *jeu d'esprit* very much of the 1920s, but still entertaining; and the recent Concerto for Two Pianos and Orchestra, quite one of his best works: its second movement is a capital set of variations, including an irresistible waltz movement.

It will already be seen that this composer can work equally happily on a small or large scale. One of the most modest, and at the same time agreeable, of his chamber works, is a Sonata for Treble Recorder, or equally Flute, and Piano. This is of moderate difficulty for both players, and forms an addition to the library of modern wind music which should not be overlooked. Outstanding among his chamber music, too, is the Trio for Violin, Viola and Cello—not an easy medium to handle—which has an especially delightful and characteristic first movement. The work has apparently been recorded in Germany, but is not available here.

When we turn to his vocal works, there is one composition which certainly should be recorded, and which must be reckoned as one of his outstanding works, namely, the *Four Poems of St Teresa of Avila,* for Contralto and Strings, first sung by Kathleen Ferrier. These show at their best Lennox Berkeley's powers of expressing his ideas seriously yet not ponderously, with attractive vocal line and very clear texture in the strings: notably the second and third songs, the former having in its sweetness a feeling of Mahler about it, seem to me exceptionally fine examples of modern English writing for solo voice.

I have left orchestral works till last, though they are certainly not the least important. Fortunately the *Divertimento* for Chamber Orchestra is available in an excellent Decca recording, and both this and the equally attractive *Serenade for Strings* are heard reasonably often in the concert hall and in broadcasts. His Symphony while obviously on a larger scale is, as one would expect from him, not by any means a work in the epic manner: its faster movements display the transparency of a Haydn symphony. The slow movement shows the deeper side of Berkeley, which possibly has become more prominent in later years; but this aspect of him is by no means incompatible with the slighter, more piquant qualities which form at least an equally characteristic part of his musical make-up.

For the last few years Berkeley, like several other British composers, has been working on an opera—his first. Conveniently enough the librettist, the well-known writer and critic Alan Pryce-Jones, had a flat in the composer's house! This proximity may have eased the composer-librettist difficulties, without which hardly an opera in history has been written. Lennox Berkeley's father was a regular Naval Officer, and the subject chosen for this opera is appropriate. At present tentatively and rather barely called *Nelson*, it deals with various episodes in his life, Lady Hamilton being an important a figure in the opera. For many years Berkeley has had a passionate interest, perhaps partly inherited, in the life of Nelson, and when a few years ago, he read the standard life by Carola Oman, he felt that this was clearly the theme for his opera. He has distinguished himself already in so many other fields of composition, instrumental and vocal alike, that I feel confident that the production of *Nelson* will be an event of considerable importance: a 'try-out' in the concert hall of substantial excerpts took place early in 1953 and did much to confirm this confidence.

XI

MICHAEL TIPPETT

(b. 1905)

A STRIKING, IF rather solitary, personality in English
musical life, Michael Tippett at the age of forty-eight
appears to be one of the least prolific of the composers described in this book. His output is perhaps to be compared
with that of his friend William Walton, three years older
than himself, though Tippett has less orchestral and—with
three string quartets—more chamber music to his credit. Both
have, at the time of writing, virtually completed their first
opera. Besides the quartets, Tippett's most notable works are
probably the Concerto for Double String Orchestra and the
oratorio *A Child of our Time*. Some would include also the
two works for voice and piano, *Boyhood's End* (words by
W. H. Hudson) and *The Heart's Assurance* (words by two
young poets who died in the last war, Alun Lewis and
Sidney Keyes), though I am inclined to rate these works,
characteristic though they are, rather less high. None of these
compositions, it is to be noted, dates from earlier than 1939,
except the First Quartet of 1935, and this was revised eight
years later. But Michael Tippett has not been quite such a
late starter as would seem to be implied, for most of his
earlier music has been set aside or scrapped.

Tippett is essentially of country rather than urban leanings.
He comes of Cornish stock, but his home for about the first
fifteen years of his life was a small village in Suffolk: later
on, after his student days, he lived in complete simplicity in
a Surrey cottage, and now he has settled in a remote part of
Sussex, near the Kent border. His musical studies were started
in earnest when he was eighteen: at the Royal College of
Music he took composition lessons under Charles Wood

and R. O. Morris, as well as studying conducting. In 1940, he was appointed Musical Director of Morley College, London, thus following in the footsteps of Gustav Holst. During his twelve years or so at Morley College, the many students who passed through his hands and sang or played under his conductorship testify to the extraordinary stimulus which Tippett offered both as a person and as a musician, with his equal enthusiasm for old and new music, his widely-ranging mind, and, at times, the unorthodoxy of his viewpoint. The public, too, has reason to be grateful to him for enabling them to hear a wealth of rarely-performed music introduced in recent years by the Morley College Concerts Society. In 1952 he resigned his post at Morley College,[1] presumably in order to devote himself entirely to composition.

The oratorio *A Child of our Time* is, excluding the opera, Tippett's biggest work to date. It was written in the first year of the war, and is based on an incident of 1938, in which a young and persecuted Jewish refugee, in despair at his inability to obtain a passport (compare *The Consul*) killed a German diplomat in Paris. This killing was followed by an appalling pogrom, and the youth, handed over to the Germans on the fall of France, was heard of no more. Tippett wrote his own text, and uses this incident symbolically to give the work a universal significance. Musically one of the most striking features of the score is the inclusion of a number of Negro spirituals, whose position in this work is not unlike that of chorales in a Bach Passion. Though some surprise and criticism were occasioned thereby when the work was first heard, the extraordinary sensitiveness and musicianship with which these spirituals are set soon convinced listeners of their appropriateness in this score, to which they make a telling emotional and dramatic contribution. In Tippett's music generally there are to be found considerable elements of jazz, the blues, and the spiritual, and there is a similarity to be noted, for example, between one of the spirituals in this work ('O by and by I'm going to lay down my heavy load') and the opening of the Concerto for Double String Orchestra.

[1] His successor is P. Racine Fricker.

If *A Child of our Time* was the first work which brought Tippett's name before a wide public, the String Concerto— a slightly earlier composition—has now become the work of his which is most frequently played: it thoroughly deserves its status in the modern repertoire of string orchestras. It is curious that it has had to wait until 1952 before finding its place in a commercial record catalogue, a place that it owes to the good offices of the British Council, under whose auspices the work has been recorded. Of its three movements, the outer ones exhibit Tippett's liking for syncopated and uneven rhythms, sometimes of a rather jerky nature. The first movement is deliberately marked eight-eight rather than two-two, because of the unequal division of the quavers in many of the bars. The last movement, which starts off in a mixture of three-four and six-eight, has a most attractive secondary tune whose rhythmic lift is caused by its construction of one bar of four-four followed by two bars of three-four. The middle, slow movement is of a warmth unusual in Tippett's music, with a suggestion of Elgar in its melodic line and of the blues in its harmonies.

Another work for strings,[1] much slighter, but still a concert work in the professional sense, is the *Little Music for String Orchestra*. This was written in 1946 for the tenth birthday of the Jacques String Orchestra, and is a neat and engaging piece of writing which deserves to be more often played. In that it is largely contrapuntal, with two fugal movements and an Air on a ground bass, it reveals Tippett's natural affinity with composers of the 17th and 18th centuries, such as Bach, Handel and Purcell, though there is nothing of the spuriously archaic in his own music. Indeed, the brisk fugal finale of this particular work, based on two intervals of the fourth, is essentially of the 20th century.

On a light level, lighter than the foregoing, is the occasional music which the B.B.C. commissioned from Tippett to celebrate the birth of Prince Charles. This orchestral suite of

[1] By the time this book is published, yet a third work for this medium will have appeared, since Tippett has been commissioned to write for the Edinburgh Festival, 1953, a set of Variations for String Orchestra on a theme by Corelli.

five movements has charm and vivacity, the former quality being especially in evidence in the Berceuse, with its haunting oboe theme, the latter in the Intrada and in the movement entitled Procession and Dance, a great deal of which is for wind and percussion only.

Neither of Tippett's two works for piano can be counted as unqualified successes, though each has its attractions and displays at least some of his characteristics. His Sonata, one of his earlier works (1937), was first played by Phyllis Sellick, to whom the other work, the Fantasia for Piano and Orchestra on a theme of Handel (1941), is dedicated. The four-movement Sonata seems rather too long for its material, especially the first movement, in which the rhythmical restlessness can become irritating. The unforced lyricism of the slow movement, and the gay syncopations of the finale provide the best music of the work. The Handel theme on which the Fantasia is based is taken from one of the Harpsichord Suites;[1] it is a theme of astonishing sweep and grandeur. Around it Tippett weaves music that is at times inventive, at times slightly laboured. It can hardly be said that in his treatment the theme grows or flowers, and it may reasonably be asked how such a theme, perfectly shaped and matured bloom as it is, could be expected to do so.

Of the three string quartets, it can briefly be said that they form an important contribution to modern English chamber music, and that the second, which is the best known by virtue of having been recorded, is the most approachable and perhaps the best: though the Third Quartet, a five-movement work lasting 35 minutes, may in the course of time—and given a recording—find an equal place in our affections. It clearly has much serious content to offer which, despite the clarity of the actual string writing, it does not readily yield.

Tippett has been working for a long time on his opera, which is entitled Midsummer Madness, the book being by himself. If it were not for the dramatic quality shown by A Child of our Time, one would hardly have thought of Tippett

---

[1] The same suite (in B flat) provided Brahms with the theme of his set of piano variations.

as an operatic composer. His vocal writing in the cantata, *Boyhood's End*, is taxing to the performer, and to some listeners may well seem over-florid. Oddly enough, the criticism of his other vocal work, *The Heart's Assurance*, is that the piano part is overloaded with notes, to which the voice part forms an uncomfortable subsidiary. Further, there is a certain emotional coolness in much of his music in which the average sensual man finds that he cannot luxuriate as he habitually likes to do—rightly or wrongly—in the theatre. Whether these criticisms are valid or not, there can be no doubt that a musical mind of Tippett's distinction is sure to be stimulated by the problems of writing for the stage, and it is to be hoped that it will not be too long before the opera is produced.

XII

ALAN RAWSTHORNE

(b. 1905)

ALAN RAWSTHORNE WAS born in the same year as his friend Constant Lambert (who conducted and recorded several of his works), and three years later than another great friend—and fellow-Lancastrian—William Walton, to whom Rawsthorne dedicated his Violin Concerto. Unlike both these friends, however, Rawsthorne was relatively late in making his mark as a composer. Previously he had toyed with architecture and had also had some training as a dentist. In the latter vocation his career was brief and unspectacular, and he can be said to have made no mark at all, figuratively speaking: while today, despite the irrefutable fact that there are too few dentists and too many composers, Rawsthorne does not practise dentistry at all, not even—as Constant Lambert once pointed out—as a hobby.

Rawsthorne had reached his early thirties before he began to attract attention in the musical world. His stature as a composer was beginning to grow when the war came (the First Piano Concerto is just pre-war, as is his notable *Symphonic Studies*), and he went into the Army: not before, however, he had lost several manuscript works in a blitz on Bristol, where he was living temporarily. (With characteristic succinctness, Rawsthorne has said that he was blown up and called up in quick succession!) Of course, his composing career was interrupted, but none the less the war was indirectly responsible for a particularly successful work of his: E.N.S.A. commissioned him to write an overture for troop concerts, and the result was the piquant *Street Corner,* which in fact is an excellent short introduction to his music.

But generally during the war he had little or no time to

compose. Occasionally, he was 'let out' to conduct. One of these occasions he has wittily and modestly described[1] when he conducted his Piano Concerto at the Promenade Concerts in 1942, with Louis Kentner as soloist:

It was the first time a work of mine had been performed at a Prom. I was nervous. I had been let out from an Army camp on an obscure Welsh mountain for forty-eight hours to come and do it. The main difficulty in conducting at concerts, I have found, is in getting yourself on to the platform in the first place, and it has been authoritatively observed that the longest distance on the surface of the earth is from the artists' room to the rostrum. This I managed to achieve, buoyed up by the reassuring presence of Mr Kentner, and gazed for a moment upon the prospect before me. I did not, like a drowning man up for the third time, review my past life. I did not even think of the Prince Consort or Sir Michael Costa. The present was quite enough . . . Actually, once you start to conduct, there is usually a certain interest in the music, even if you have written it yourself, which keeps your mind from preying upon the more gruesome side of things.

Since the end of the war Rawsthorne has been writing, steadily if not prolifically, works which have put him right into the forefront of contemporary composers. From 1948 onwards he has produced among other music a Violin Concerto, a Quartet for Clarinet and Strings, a Cello Sonata, a Concerto for String Orchestra, a Symphony and a Second Piano Concerto, each one of which is an outstanding achievement in its particular medium.

Before talking about these and other works of his, let me say something of the man, for there are aspects of his personality which can be equated with characteristics of his music—such is by no means always the case. His somewhat dry humour comes through in his music, and so does his love for quiet understatement rather than the reverse. He is generally a reticent person, occasionally forthright, as a Lancashire man should be. He has a hatred of pomposity, whether in a person or in a work of art. He is fastidious,

---

[1] In an introductory essay which Rawsthorne wrote to the Prom. Syllabus of 1949.

discriminating, and deliberate rather than precipitate in both his life and his work. The always companionable exterior manner, his charm, urbanity and wit, tend to cover up an innate and intense seriousness which runs parallel with these other qualities. The same parallel is observable in his music.

One of the most remarkable virtues of his music is the actual handling of the orchestra. He seems to think in terms of orchestral instruments, and what he writes for them is faultlessly and gratefully shaped for the instrument or instruments in question. I suspect that he learned an immense amount in this respect, not from text-books on orchestration, but from his friendship with professional orchestral players. From them, too, he has picked up the rather baffling terminology they use in conversation. For example, a 45-minute symphony is known, rather optimistically, as a tune; any woodwind instrument is referred to as a flute; any stringed instrument as a fiddle; a wrong note is a domino, and, most curious of all, a commonplace ending in C major is a browning.

Perhaps the best example I can recommend to demonstrate this orchestral assurance and polish on Rawsthorne's part is his *Symphonic Studies*. This is one of his finest works and fortunately is recorded (by H.M.V. under British Council auspices). It consists of five studies written around a central theme and broken up by re-statements of that theme. One's attention is immediately captured by the broad and impressive, almost Beethoven-like introduction which leads into the allegro theme. The studies that follow show both variety and balance, alternating between moods of amiable briskness and of gentle, reflective melancholy: the latter is extremely characteristic of, and personal to, Rawsthorne and it is a mood recurrent in all his work. *Symphonic Studies*, however, ends on a cheerful note: after an exhilarating fugato towards the end, starting most strikingly on trombone and percussion, the music takes on more and more vigour and virtuosity. The final bar is a triple forte B major chord for brass, with no nonsense about it.

Another orchestral piece which I have mentioned, also

recorded, is the *Street Corner* overture. Without any trace of conscious 'writing down', Rawsthorne here produced a thoroughly popular work which subsequent concert audiences have continued to enjoy as much as the original army audiences did. Again, as in *Symphonic Studies,* the music represents a wide range of moods, such as can be encountered at any crossroads of the imaginary busy industrial town which gives the clue to the title. Sometimes there are strident bursts of sound, at other times one overhears whispered snatches of conversation. Even in so slight a work, one notices—I wonder whether the troops did—a good deal of the imitational devices for which Rawsthorne has a predilection.

Though I have laid stress on Rawsthorne's skill and resourcefulness in handling the orchestra, his music does not depend for effect solely upon the colours which instrumental timbres supply. One of his most successful recent works is the Concerto for Strings only. Here, in this somewhat severe work, it is purely the force and logic of the musical reasoning that carries the listener along. Its middle, slow movement shows strongly that serious reflective mood which I have remarked upon as being very typical of him: the movement has indeed been christened by musicians as 'melancholy variations upon "God Save the Queen"', which it resembles thematically!

To turn to a gayer and lighter work, there is the First Piano Concerto. As a student at the Royal Manchester College of Music, Rawsthorne took piano as one of his studies and he continued it abroad under Egon Petri. Though he has never considered himself to rate as a public performer, undoubtedly these studies were valuable in giving him an understanding of keyboard writing. His piano music, in fact, shows an expertness in its layout and registration which is not universal among modern English composers. It is delicate yet satisfying writing, as this Piano Concerto shows, avoiding both the lushness of the Tchaikovsky-Rachmaninov imitators and, at the other extreme, the miserably thin, scratching sounds of the 'austerity' school of modern piano-composers (what sins of ungraciousness are committed these days in the name of 'economy'). Of the Piano Concerto's three move-ments, the first, entitled Capriccio, gives the soloist plenty of rapid *bravura* passages, and also contains a very characteristic second subject—a march-like tune, yet hardly military, first heard on the bassoon, and rather reminding one of Prokofiev. The central Chaconne is a most appealing movement, notice-able for its constantly shifting harmonic scheme—again, a characteristic of this composer and one which gives his music a somewhat restless feeling. The final Tarantella shows further evidence of this quality. It is a delicate rather than boisterous affair, requiring very clean playing. It ends *sempre ppp* which is possibly one reason why the work has not quite attained the popularity of certain war-horses in the piano concerto repertory!

The Second Piano Concerto of 1951 is a rather more sub-stantial work and more of a pianist's work. It is probably Rawsthorne's best composition to date and has, moreover, had the advantage of a soloist of superb distinction in Clifford Curzon, for whom it was written. Each of its four movements is attractive, the first delicate, the second in con-trast an aggressive scherzo, the third a deeply original slow movement in which one sees more and more as one gets to know it, the last the gayest of finales with a catchy tune which one cannot help whistling in a quite maddening way!

Besides two Concertos he has composed three shorter works for piano.[1] The set of *Four Bagatelles*, recorded by Denis Matthews, is well worth looking at. It is not exceptionally difficult, especially the second piece, a type of Siciliano, which for the pianist is perhaps the best introduction to the parti-cular flavour of Rawsthorne's style. A later Piano Sonatina, though it repays study, *is* difficult and is not outstanding among his recent output. Finally, Rawsthorne has most happily catered for those who play duets at one piano, an enjoyable and profitable recreation which I sincerely hope is not dying out. The work in question is a Suite called, after Izaak Walton, *The Creel*, and one does not need to have

[1] He has since written a set of Romantic Pieces for piano, dedicated to Frank Merrick who first peformed them in March 1953.

piscatorial habits to enjoy the neat wit of this music. Each of the four short pieces has a descriptive quotation as title: 'The Mighty *Pike* is the Tyrant of the Fresh Water'; 'The *Sprat*—a Fish that is ever in Motion' (this is an exact, and very rapid, canon throughout): 'The *Carp* is the Queen of Rivers—a stately, a Good, and a very Subtil Fish' (even players of a most humble attainment can tackle this piece): and 'The Leap or Summersault of the *Salmon*'.

It will have been observed from this survey that Rawsthorne is primarily an instrumental rather than a vocal composer, though he has written a few songs and, in 1952, his first choral essay, *A Canticle of Man*, for baritone, mixed chorus, flute, and strings. He has also been responsible for a considerable amount of film music (one of his best recent scores in this medium was to *The Cruel Sea*). Whether in film or concert music, Rawsthorne seems to me a most distinctive figure in English music—one has only to hear a few consecutive bars in the concert hall or the cinema to know that the composer is Rawsthorne, and no one else. The influences which one can detect are slight; I have mentioned Prokofiev, and one could perhaps add Roussel and, occasionally, Hindemith. But these influences amount to little. His voice is refreshingly his own.

XIII

CONSTANT LAMBERT

(1905-1951)

IN THE 1920s, two young English composers appeared on the contemporary scene. They caused more than the usual stir, firstly because there was a dearth of new talent in that field at the time, and secondly, because *their* talent was clearly exceptional. They were William Walton and Constant Lambert, born respectively in 1902 and 1905. Both fulfilled their early promise, Walton exclusively as a composer, Lambert in at least two other directions besides composition. These two brilliant young men were naturally coupled with each other directly they began to come before the public, in the same rather arbitrary way that, for example, the names of Debussy and Ravel were joined together, and with no more intrinsic reason. Their subsequent careers did not run on parallel lines, but they remained the firmest of friends: Lambert conducted and recorded much of Walton's music, and was closely associated as narrator with what is probably Walton's best-known work, the *Façade Entertainment*.

Already you begin to see the many-sidedness of Lambert—conductor, narrator, composer, and as we shall remark later, one of the most shrewd and biting writers upon the music of the present time. In this country we tend to distrust versatility. We argue, for instance, that one person cannot be both a first-class executant and a first-class composer, forgetting the examples of the numerous keyboard-executant-composers of the past, from Bach onwards. So I believe that, if Constant Lambert's merits as a composer are perhaps undervalued, and if some of his works are less heard than they might be, it is because of his achievement in other branches of music, especially of course as conductor. Furthermore, it follows that the time he spent in studying scores and rehearsing and giving concerts had to be subtracted from the time he devoted to composition; and at the best of times he was not a quick composer.

Lambert was born in London, the son of a painter, the late G. W. Lambert, A.R.A.; his brother is the well-known sculptor, Maurice Lambert, A.R.A. Constant Lambert himself had an extremely penetrating appreciation of the pictorial arts, which stood him in particularly good stead in the artistic posts he held in the world of ballet. It was in that world that, after general education at Christ's Hospital, and while still a student at the Royal College of Music, he first made his mark—and in a truly notable way. His exceptional gifts came to the attention of no less a person than Diaghilev, who paid him the distinction, unique among English composers, of commissioning a ballet from him for the famous company bearing his name. This was *Romeo and Juliet*, produced in 1926 at Monte Carlo. His second ballet, *Pomona*, was produced by Nijinska at Buenos Aires in the following year.

When the English Sadler's Wells Ballet was formed, soon after Diaghilev's death and the consequent disintegration of his company, the twenty-five-year-old Constant Lambert was appointed as its Musical Director: he remained so for some sixteen years, later becoming Artistic Director. He had all the necessary special qualifications which made him the ideal person for the post, and it is impossible to over-estimate the importance of the part played by this one man, musically and artistically, in the establishment of an English school of ballet. Among his qualifications, one can mention that, from his early days, he had played the piano for ballet rehearsals and performances (incidentally he again took his place at the piano in touring ballets during the orchestra-less days of the last war); his conducting technique had just the right combination of precision and plasticity; his own compositions have, above all, a direct rhythmic appeal, particularly noticeable in his ballet music. And I have already referred to his insight

F

into the pictorial arts—not common among musicians, just as painters tend to have little ear for music. It is no wonder that he never tired of his early love for ballet: his last work, completed shortly before his tragically early death in 1951, was the ballet *Tiresias,* commissioned by the Arts Council and produced at Covent Garden with choreography by Frederick Ashton.

Lambert was always, with his many activities, a busy man in music. He had few hobbies: they are said to have included playing Russian billiards and composing limericks, of which he had a vast and distinguished collection. If you look him up in *Who's Who in Music* you will see that he was President of the Kensington Cats' Club, thus revealing another 'hobby'—though this is an inadequate word to describe the passionate devotion he had for members of the feline population, a devotion which other composers, including notably the late Peter Warlock, have shared. Lambert's other likes included the music of Sousa and Duke Ellington, the Zoo, Marx Brothers' films, good food and drink, and what goes with good food and drink—good conversation. He was wedded to London, with a partiality towards the Regent's Park area and Camden Town (a neighbourhood made famous by the painter Sickert, and still possessing its special atmosphere).

Lambert's last published work, *Trois Pièces Nègres,* bears at the end the words 'Camden Town—Palermo, 1949', a designation which not merely pleased his taste for the curious, but which also happened to be true, since the composition of the work was divided between these two distant and contrasted places. As for his taste for the curious, he revealed something of this in most diverting articles for *Lilliput*: I recall one dealing with the odd assortment of objects that one unwittingly acquires in bidding for a lot at an auction sale; another on the peculiarity of indexes; and he was always adding with glee to his anthology (for private circulation only) of examples of people talking at cross-purposes. He was Francophile in his nature and this was reflected in many of the programmes he conducted, which contained a good proportion of French music, Chabrier and Satie being especial favourites.

Of his own compositions, one has proved enormously popular, though this was against the expectations of the composer. I refer to *The Rio Grande*. Because of its unusual scoring (for solo piano, chorus, strings, brass including cornets as well as trumpets, lots of percussion, but no woodwind) the composer told me that he never thought the work would have more than a mere handful of performances—whereas, in fact, during the ten years following its première in 1929, it had about two hundred performances, and it still keeps its place. The occasion of its first production in 1929 was a notable one, since Lambert himself conducted, and the solo piano part was played by Sir Hamilton Harty. The work was recorded by them at the time, but a new recording has appeared, again with Lambert conducting, with the young artist Kyla Greenbaum as the solo pianist. This setting of Sacheverell Sitwell's colourful poem could not have remained in the repertoire as it has done if it had been just a curiosity, a piece of highbrow jazz and nothing more. It has indeed become a *locus classicus* for the use of jazz in serious music, but the work is, in addition, a beautifully made composition with its careful balance of vigorous rhythmic sections and passages of quiet, warm, lyrical writing. *The Rio Grande* has also achieved considerable success as a ballet.

Lambert's music generally makes frequent use of syncopated rhythms, but not usually the syncopations of jazz. There are, none the less, jazzy episodes in works other than *The Rio Grande,* especially 'blues' passages. One of his early piano works is, in fact, entitled *Elegiac Blues* (dedicated to the memory of the coloured revue actress, Florence Mills): and there are blues passages in both the Piano Sonata—not, I think, one of his best works—and the Concerto for Piano and Nine Instruments.

Syncopated rhythms, too, you will find in his *Trois Pièces Nègres pour les Touches Blanches*—a characteristic title— excellent fun to play and, if you are not daunted by the rhythmic traps, not too difficult: it is for one piano, four hands, a welcome addition to the repertoire of this once popular medium. Another playable (solo) piano piece is the charming *Siciliana,* taken from the early ballet I have mentioned above, *Pomona.*

Of his orchestral works, there is a most attractive Suite from the later ballet *Horoscope,* which is recorded. I particularly commend to the listener the captivating Valse and the Finale ('Invocation to the Moon')—the latter has a richness and theatrical effectiveness about it which makes one think perhaps of Puccini, and why not? Then there is the quiet *Aubade Héroique* for small orchestra, dedicated to Ralph Vaughan Williams on his seventieth birthday. The composer has written at the beginning of the score—'This short piece was inspired by a daybreak during the invasion of Holland, the calm of the surrounding park contrasting with the distant mutterings of war.' The explanation of this note is that Lambert was in Holland with the Sadler's Wells Ballet at the beginning of the war, and was caught there by the German invasion.

Lambert worked comparatively little for films, though his score to *Anna Karenina* was a distinguished feature of the film: from another film comes the Concert Suite entitled *Merchant Seamen.*

There are two choral works to mention, one a fairly straightforward setting of the *Dirge* from Shakespeare's *Cymbeline,* for male voices and strings; the other was certainly his most extended and I think most important work, namely *Summer's Last Will and Testament,* a Masque for baritone solo, chorus and orchestra, the words taken from the play of this name written in 1593 by Thomas Nashe. There are seven movements in this work, two of them being purely orchestral. One of these, the *Rondo Burlesca* ('King Pest') is heard occasionally in the concert hall on its own, and is a kind of brilliant English equivalent of Dukas's *L'Apprenti Sorcier.* The poems set include the well-known 'Spring, the Sweet Spring', and the work ends with a most moving setting, in Saraband form, of the poem beginning—

Adieu, farewell earth's bliss!
This world uncertain is:
Fond are life's lustful joys,
Death proves them all but toys.
None from his darts can fly;
I am sick, I must die—
Lord, have mercy on us!

I have referred above, briefly, to Lambert's ability as a writer upon music. His book, *Music Ho!* is a most stimulating and trenchant study of contemporary music: it is available cheaply in the Pelican edition, and wonderful value it is. No one can fail to enjoy it, even if he may—as I do—disagree with some of the controversial views which Lambert put forward, but even where one disagrees, one still realises the penetration of an extraordinarily acute, critical mind. Lambert was not impressed by so-called 'revolutions' in contemporary musical language, and I may suitably end this article by quoting a few sentences from his book, dealing with this point:

There is nothing in music which has really lost its meaning, no device of rhythm, no harmonic combination which the composer of vision cannot re-animate.

The music of the future, if it is to avoid the many psychological cul-de-sacs which have been examined in this volume, must inevitably be directed towards a new angle of vision rather than to the exploitation of a new vocabulary.

XIV

HERBERT MURRILL

(1909-1952)

WITHIN A YEAR of the death of Constant Lambert, English musical life sustained a second loss, which it could ill afford, of a musician under the age of fifty. Both were versatile rather than specialist musicians. Herbert Murrill was a skilled organist and pianist, a sympathetic and stimulating teacher, the shrewdest of critics on the rare occasions when he wrote about music, a composer of considerable charm, and an outstanding success as Head of Music at the B.B.C. I doubt if I have ever met, and known closely, a more vivacious person, but I must make a reservation that his particular brand of vivacity was of the quiet and polished variety rather than the boisterous. We shall see that these qualities of polish and of vivacity are evident in his music. He was the wittiest of conversationalists, with a gift for precise expression; a devastating mimic of other people's peculiarities of speaking; and he had a fund of stories and memories of odd experiences, sometimes ridiculous, sometimes inclining to the gruesome, with which to regale you. Although his manner was easy and friendly, he was not perhaps as sociable as one expected him to be. He was happier talking to one or two people only or—better still—indulging in his favourite pastime of strumming at the piano the music he liked. He would spend an entire evening like this, working through an immense pile of music—he sight-read with extreme fluency.

Herbert Murrill was only forty-three when he died and he had already had one of the busiest and varied of musical careers. He studied at the Royal Academy under York Bowen and Alan Bush, and under Sir Hugh Allen and Dr Ernest

Walker at Oxford, where he was organ scholar at Worcester College and President of the University Musical Club, and where he took the degrees of M.A. and B.Mus. Soon after he came down from Oxford he became a professor of composition at the Royal Academy of Music and took on also an organist's post at a London church.

He joined the B.B.C. in 1936, and was in Army Intelligence during the war. On demobilisation he returned to the B.B.C. and became Assistant Head of Music. He was appointed Head of Music in succession to Sir Steuart Wilson in 1950.

Up to his death he still held his professorship at the Royal Academy of Music and I once questioned him on how he set about teaching that virtually unteachable subject, composition. His remarks, in particular two cardinal points that he made, have stuck in my mind and will not, I think, be out of place in this book. Firstly, Murrill insisted that his pupil must *think* hard about what he is doing, must indeed think why he is writing music at all. As Murrill put it, 'composing music is neither an easy nor a profitable thing to do' and an aspiring composer should not therefore idly indulge in covering sheets of manuscript paper with black and white symbols. He must have a compelling and engrossing urge to do so. Secondly, Murrill insisted on the need for discipline—the shapeless torrent of ideas must be controlled ('corseted' was Murrill's own and singularly apt word). Technique, whether that of the sixteenth or eighteenth century, or the Schoenbergian 12-note system of this century, has always been used to canalise composers' thoughts, so that the shapeless torrent becomes a precise and directed jet.

It was very interesting to me, knowing that Murrill had no great love for the more doctrinaire aspects of the Schoenberg school of composition, to note that he did occasionally find it helpful for a pupil to be introduced to this technique of writing; one cannot be arbitrary, he felt, in prescribing this or that system as the only framework in which a pupil is to write—what may suit and help one struggling composer may make another even more frustrated. In any case Murrill wrote a warning,[1] *à propos* 12-note technique, but equally applicable to other techniques:

It must be emphasised that no system will actually do the composer's work. He (poor wretch) still has to write music—to arrange his sounds in significant order—whatever system he chooses to adopt. Schoenberg has been called—cruelly enough—the Ebenezer Prout of the twelve-tonalists. We may deplore the cruelty of the remark, yet heed its warning. Where the disciples of Prout were chastised with whips, those of Schœnberg are chastised with scorpions; yet an uninspired and slavish following of Schœnberg's rules will no more automatically produce music than a dovout and humble acceptance of Prout's.

So much for some of Murrill's ideas on the composition of music, the ideas clearly of one who practised and thought very seriously about the art. In modern English music I get the impression that he rated Vaughan Williams and Walton very high, in foreign music he gravitated strongly towards the French school and to Stravinsky. But while he was sympathetic to *all* contemporary music, of whatever nationality, he was acutely critical and discriminating, and by no means lavish in praise. He had the honesty to dislike even when he was against the majority view in so doing.

It is time to talk of Murrill's own music. Because of his many-sided activities he had less time to devote to composition than many of us wished. But this was not the only reason why the majority of his works were on a smaller rather than an epic scale. For he felt an aversion towards the epic: his instinctive love was for modern French music—its piquant harmony; its occasional leaning towards the music-hall tune and the rhythm as well as the harmony of dance music; its clarity and, above all, its logical order and neat finish—all these characteristics tell throughout his own music. There are no loose ends. Ravel perhaps is the figure who stands over—and surely would have approved—what is one of the few examples of Murrill's extended works and certainly his best, his String Quartet. It is a four-movement

[1] In *Music Today* (Dennis Dobson, Ltd.)

work of not excessive difficulty for the players. The second movement is an outstandingly good Scherzo, the slow movement has a warmth and ripeness somewhat rare in Murrill's music. And the syncopated finale has a verve about it that only the stuffiest audience would fail to enjoy.

Another full-scale work heard in London before the war was a Cello Concerto, which he subsequently decided was unsatisfactory and withdrew. Some fifteen years later he was commissioned by the Henry Wood Concerts Society to write a second Cello Concerto, and this was first performed at the Albert Hall in 1951, the soloist being his wife Vera Canning, one of the most distinguished of our younger cellists. The work is attractive, concise, and original in form. Murrill has epitomised the features of the four movements of a concerto into one continuous piece, which lasts only about seventeen minutes. The haunting slow section is based on a Catalan folk song, which is known to possess a particular significance for Casals. It was Casals who drew Murrill's attention to the tune, and it is to him that the Concerto is dedicated, 'with respect and affection'. Murrill wrote other smaller works for the cello which are both useful and likable. They include a Capriccio in three movements and 'Four French Nursery Songs', freely and Gallicly set.

I have said that Murrill played the piano well, and it is an instrument which he really understood. He wrote a fair number of shorter piano pieces, mostly fairly difficult. But the reasonably deft student will enjoy, for example, his *Caprice on Two Norfolk Folk Tunes,* the tunes being 'Green Broom' and 'Twenty Eighteen'; or the two short, cleverly imitative Impromptus, *Hommage à Chopin* and *Hommage à Poulenc.* Also perfectly playable on the piano, though written for the harpsichord, is the *Suite Française*—you notice constantly the Gallic affinities—consisting of three different types of Air, namely, 'Gai', 'Sérieux', 'Champêtre', which are sandwiched between an opening 'Prélude et Fughette' and a 'Final'. The Sonatina for Piano is quite manageable and each of its three movements has its attractions: the first gaily syncopated, the second a weaving Bach-like aria, the third crisp and clear as Scarlatti. Brilliant but really difficult are the three concert pieces *Toccatina, Canzona* and *Presto Alla Giga.*

An orchestral work that occurs from time to time as a leavening element in orchestral programmes is a set of Three Hornpipes, one of them written as long ago as the late 1920s, the others added in 1932, and the whole having received its first performance at a Promenade Concert two years later. The first two recall characteristics of the eighteenth-century type of hornpipe, while the third is a highly stylised twentieth-century affair, a hornpipe in spirit rather than form: three-four and three-eight bars alternate with two-four, and the trickiness of the rhythms rather reminds one of Walton's *Portsmouth Point.*

Two works dated 1950 need to be mentioned; a Sonata for treble recorder (or flute) and harpsichord written for Carl Dolmetsch, one of Murrill's happiest inventions; and a 'Handelian Fragment' entitled *Humpty Dumpty* for voice and piano. As to the latter I need only quote part of the editorial note printed in the score:

It is impossible, from a right reading of the internal evidence, to avoid the conclusion that this charming Aria is from the pen of Handel, and that it dated from the year 1714 or 1715.

The legendary figure of Humpty Dumpty may be taken to represent the composer himself; a glance at any contemporary portrait would suggest as much. 'Sitting on the wall' may be taken variously as having reference to Handel's elevated social position (for he had been patronised by Lord Burlington, lived at his house in Piccadilly, and had written an Ode for the Birthday of Queen Anne) or alternatively may allude to his precarious situation when his former patron, The Elector of Hanover, became George I of England. His loss of Royal favour, since he had overstayed the Elector's leave, is of course the 'great fall' of which the poem speaks.

The music that follows is a most delightful parody, and it seems that Murrill's gift for mimicry covered composers' styles as well as his friends' mannerisms of speech. Perhaps it is fitting to end this survey of his music with these remarks about a pure piece of fun, rather than with a heavy-going analysis of a four-movement symphony.

Murrill's work, cut short as it was and in any case small in quantity because he wrote slowly and with almost excessive care and patience, struck a fresh note in English music. The best tribute we can pay to so brilliantly gifted and nimble a mind is to continue to perform its essentially enjoyable products.

XV

BENJAMIN BRITTEN

(b. 1913)

IT IS A fact, and one surely to be deplored, that the
majority of younger English composers—as distinct from
their seniors—have written little or no music for schools and
young people. Look through the output of such composers
as Walton, Rubbra, Rawsthorne, Berkeley, Tippett, Lambert,
for example, and you will find very little indeed that can be
said to come into this category. The reasons for this abstin-
ence are no concern of the present article, which *is* con-
cerned with the one major exception, Benjamin Britten; for
Britten, in several works and in several different ways, has
put all young persons in this country deeply in his debt. It is
not altogether surprising that he should have interested himself in providing music for youth. Britten himself has been
called 'a poet of childhood'[1] and, despite the fact that as a
composer he reached maturity at an early age, he still retains
many of the characteristics of youth. His boyish appearance,
the open-air clothes that he wears, and above all his zest
and enthusiasm, combine to deceive one into putting his age
considerably lower than it is—until one remembers his enormous achievements in the art of music.

Britten works quickly: or rather, he writes his music down
quickly, having done most of the composing in his mind
before committing a note to paper. Like Mozart, one imagines
that Britten is quite capable of writing a prelude down while
simultaneously composing the ensuing fugue. This facility, a
quick understanding for the practical problems of the medium
for which he is writing, and the positive delight he takes in a
medium of limited resources, have made Britten more than

[1] In an article in *Vogue* in 1951 by Edward Sackville-West.

usually adept in providing occasional music for schools and amateur performers. He can look back, in his own case, to very juvenile experiences in music. Born (at Lowestoft) on the Suffolk coast which has remained a steadfast love of his—three of his operas are actually set in Suffolk—he learned to play both piano and viola before most of us learn to read. It is of interest to note that today he is a masterly pianist and accompanist of singers, possessing a quite extraordinary delicacy and beauty of touch. As for the other instrument of his childhood days, I cannot say how proficient he is today on the viola, for my knowledge of his playing is limited, literally, to one note! The curious may hear Benjamin Britten playing that one note, on second viola, throughout the Purcell *Five-Part Fantasia upon One Note,* which he recorded with the Zorian Quartet for H.M.V.

But it was not only piano and viola which engaged Britten's attention at a tender age. From his fifth birthday, he was plunging earnestly into composition. He has recalled in a broadcast talk the memory of these juvenilia, or 'infantilia':
'I remember the first time I tried, the result looked rather like the Forth Bridge—in other words, hundreds of dots all over the page connected by long lines all joined together in beautiful curves. I am afraid it was the pattern on the paper which I was interested in; and when I asked my mother to play it, her look of horror upset me considerably. My next efforts were much more conscious of sound. I had started playing the piano and wrote elaborate tone poems usually lasting about twenty seconds, inspired by terrific events in my home life.'

There is one further link with these early days. In 1934, Britten's *Simple Symphony* was published with the following prefatory note:

This 'Simple Symphony' is entirely based on material from works which the composer wrote between the ages of nine and twelve. Although the development of these themes is in many places quite new, there are large stretches of the work which are taken bodily from the early pieces—save for the re-scoring for strings.

The movements of this most attractive and straightforward work, which incidentally can be played by either string orchestra or string quartet, have the titles *Boisterous Bourrée, Playful Pizzicato, Sentimental Saraband, Frolicsome Finale.*

In the same year appeared *Friday Afternoons,* a set of twelve school songs published in two volumes and forming one of the brightest and most delightful compositions for school choirs which has been written in our time. Though I cannot imagine that there are many schools in the country which do not at least know of these songs, it may be permitted perhaps to recall some of the titles. There is a simple setting of Thackeray's *A Tragic Story* ('There lived a Sage in days of yore') in G minor, with an attractively vacillating B flat and B natural. Rather more difficult is the *Fishing Song,* with words by Izaak Walton, in five-eight time (many years later Britten was to show ordinary people to their surprise that they could indeed sing without difficulty in five-time, in one of the Audience Songs in *Let's Make an Opera*). Then there is the setting of Eleanor Farjeon's *Jazz-Man,* with a tricky and exciting piano part. The majority of these songs, by the way, are in unison, but the setting of *Cuckoo* has an optional second part, and the whole collection ends with one of the best songs of all, which divides into four parts. This is a setting of *Old Abram Brown is Dead and Gone,* which must be extremely amusing to sing. It starts off as a two-part canon, then becomes a four-part canon, and ends with one group of singers delivering the tune in augmentation in crotchets, while at the same time the other group is singing it in its original form in quavers.

There are also canons to be found, of an equally un-academic nature, in Britten's three two-part songs for boys' or female voices, to words by Walter de la Mare. The first of these, *The Ride-by-Nights,* is in strict canon practically throughout. These part-songs are none too easy, but they are exciting to bring off and repay trouble spent on them.

Early in 1939 Britten went to America, with some intention in his mind to become an American citizen, as his friend and librettist W. H. Auden had done. If war had not broken out, and this intention had been fulfilled, one can only speculate as to how Britten's career would have differed from the course it has in fact taken (and speculate on other matters too—no English Opera Group, no Aldeburgh Festival?). But war did break out and Britten soon took the decision to return to England. He sailed back early in 1942 and wrote two works on the Atlantic crossing. The first of these was a setting of Auden's words, *Hymn to St Cecilia*, for unaccompanied mixed voices. It may be added here that St Cecilia's Day—St Cecilia being the Patron Saint of Music—is also Britten's birthday, November 22nd. The second of the two works was the beautifully written *Ceremony of Carols*, a sequence of original carols for treble voices, usually in three parts, accompanied by harp (or piano). The words mainly come from medieval sources. Among the many attractive pieces in this work are the brisk *Wolcum Yole*, and *Deo Gracias* ('Adam lay ibounden') with an attractive syncopation. Of the slower and gentler settings, mention must be made of *There is no Rose*, in which Britten shows his particular art of doing fresh and original things with common chords.

I have referred to the Aldeburgh Festival. This Suffolk coastal resort of 2,500 inhabitants is where Britten now lives: he moved into a house there from the converted windmill which he had occupied up to 1947 at Snape, a village about five miles inland. In 1948 he initiated the Aldeburgh Festival, and in its opening year his Cantata *Saint Nicolas* was given for the first time. A month or so later it was performed again at Lancing College, Sussex, for whose centenary celebrations it had been composed. There it was sung by the combined choirs of three boys' schools (forming the main SATB chorus), and one girls' school forming a separate 'Gallery Choir'. The accompaniment is for piano duet, organ, strings and percussion, and in a prefatory note in the score Britten points out that the string parts are 'not very sophisticated, and can be played by amateur players', while the piano duet part is also of only moderate difficulty. On the other hand, the solo tenor part of Saint Nicolas needs an outstandingly good singer of the calibre of Peter Pears, who sang it at these performances. Saint Nicolas was born in Asia Minor and died in the first half of the fourth century. He is the Patron Saint of children, seamen and travellers, and there are many popular legends about him. This Cantata is broken into several separate movements which have sub-titles, such as: 'The Birth of Nicolas' (in which a solo boy's voice, to be sung by the youngest boy in the choir, is used several times with touching effect); 'Nicolas devotes himself to God' (tenor solo); 'He Journeys to Palestine'; 'Nicolas is chosen Bishop' (ending with the first of two Hymns in which the audience-congregation joins—'All People that on Earth do dwell'); and so on, with a final number entitled 'The Death of Nicolas', ending with the second Hymn, 'God Moves in a Mysterious Way'.

The excellent text of Saint Nicolas was written by Eric Crozier, with whom Britten was to collaborate again a year later in the well-known *Let's Make an Opera.* This consists of an entertainment for young people in two parts: the first section takes the form of a play, illustrating the preparation and rehearsing of an opera, in which, writes the author, 'it is essential that real children should play the children's parts'. The second part is the opera itself, entitled *The Little Sweep,* with accompaniment for solo string quartet, piano duet and percussion, the string parts not being very easy. If necessary, the work can be done with piano duet, with or without per-cussion. In the course of this miniature opera there are four songs which, having been rehearsed beforehand, are sung by the whole audience under the direction of the conductor, and most attractive and entertaining they are. One of them, indeed, the 'Night Song', in a gentle six-eight rhythm, is one of the most enchanting tunes that Britten has ever composed. But the whole entertainment is so full of delights that they cannot be enumerated here.

In one other fairly recent work (1946) Britten has shown his interest in musical education, in a far from forbidding way. This is the work variously entitled *The Young Person's Guide to the Orchestra* or *Variations and Fugue on a Theme of*

Purcell, with a spoken commentary. It was originally written for the film, *The Instruments of the Orchestra,* and its objective is to introduce young people to the different instruments in turn. The theme of Purcell is played first by the whole orchestra and then by each one of the four sections of the orchestra—strings, woodwind, brass, percussion. Subsequent variations introduce each individual instrument and the work ends with a quite overwhelming fugue for the entire orchestra, a positive riot of sound.

In this survey I have dealt so far only with works designed for performance either by or to the young. I hope that Britten will continue to write such works. I feel sure that he will, for his enjoyment is evident on every page of them, just as it is in his use of children's choir in the *Spring Symphony.* These works for young people are in their category just as important as, for instance, his magnificent operatic contributions are in their field. It is not possible here to discuss his operas in any detail, nor perhaps is it necessary, since much has been written on them elsewhere. If *Peter Grimes,* with its exceptionally good libretto by Montagu Slater, remains in most people's view the most successful of his operas, though his first,[1] the highest praise must be given to the score of *The Rape of Lucretia.* Some portions of Ronald Duncan's text may be open to criticism, but in no other opera, not even *Grimes,* has Britten been so consistently inventive, and his musical construction so firmly planned and executed. The opera contains also one of his most beautiful pieces of writing for solo voice, the Lullaby in Act II ('She Sleeps as a Rose'). *Lucretia* was followed by a complete contrast—the comic opera, *Albert Herring,* again with book by Eric Crozier. His next opera, *Billy Budd,* was a return to tragedy. The book was adapted by E. M. Forster and Eric Crozier from a story of Herman Melville. Despite a number of brilliant musical ideas, and despite the touching lyricism of the last act, the opera as a whole was uneven. His most recent Coronation opera, *Gloriana,* has a book by William

---

[1] Excluding the operetta *Paul Bunyan,* unpublished and unperformed here.

G

Plomer, dealing with the story of Elizabeth and Essex. Despite brilliant things in the score, again this opera is something of a disappointment. But the term is relative: Britten's operatic work, regarded as a whole, remains of supreme importance in the history of twentieth-century music, and is rightly judged as such in opera-houses throughout the world.

Note: I am greatly indebted, for information used in this chapter, to the valuable little book on Britten by Eric Walter White, published by Boosey & Hawkes.

XVI

A MISCELLANEOUS GROUP
OF COMPOSERS

Humphrey Searle (b. 1915); Elisabeth Lutyens (b. 1906);
Elizabeth Maconchy (b. 1907); Benjamin Frankel (b. 1906);
Alan Bush (b. 1900); P. Racine Fricker (b. 1920)

THE FIFTEEN COMPOSERS I have discussed in the
previous chapters represent, as the reader will have
realised, a variety of styles which have little in common. A few
can be bracketed together, it is true—Bax, Ireland, Moeran
as exponents of the older type of romanticism: Berkeley and
Murrill as inclining towards a Gallic shade of thought. But
in the main it is variety rather than any basic unity which
marks the considerable total achievement of these composers,
and this is not unexpected, since the English genius prefers
to be capricious rather than regimented. It has already been
pointed out that if, in the early part of this century, it was
possible to discern a characteristically national style of composing—at least one knew roughly what one meant by des-
cribing a piece as 'typically English' or 'in the English tradition'—that is no longer possible. The composers introduced in
this chapter are similarly a 'group' only in the sense that
they are placed together for reasons of convenience in plan-
ning this book, and not for reasons connected with their
music. These composers contribute still further to the diversity of style that has so far been revealed, a diversity in which
perhaps the only noticeable gap has been that of twelve-note
music. It should not be assumed, however, that this method
of composition has left the British composer untouched. It
has attracted, as in every country, and especially in the last
decade or so, several composers here, some gifted, others

99

(less gifted) hoping to ride to renown on a bandwaggon which they wrongly imagine will camouflage their comparative lack of talent. Two English composers of undoubted distinction who have found in the twelve-note idiom an entirely congenial mode of expression, and of expressiveness, are Humphrey Searle and Elisabeth Lutyens: both use the twelve-note method with considerable freedom.

HUMPHREY SEARLE, who studied in London with John Ireland and in Vienna with Anton Webern, is the more expansive and romantically inclined. Works such as the large-scale Piano Concerto (1944) and the *Ballade for Piano* (1947) showed great imaginative quality, combined with ability to think on broad, sweeping lines. The latent powers of a serious and thoroughly musical mind have come to full fruition in the more recent *Poem for Twenty-Two Strings*, an excellently constructed lyrical essay, and the Piano Sonata of 1951. The latter was written to celebrate the 140th anniversary of the birthday of Liszt, and in the composer's words 'the music attempts to combine the Lisztian idea of thematic transformation with the twelve-note method of Schoenberg, which is of course also to make use of thematic transformation, though in a rather different way'. This one-movement work, not at all easy to play, was the first work of Searle's to be commercially recorded.

Latterly, Humphrey Searle has become more and more interested in experimenting with the tricky problems of combining the spoken voice with instruments. His *Gold Coast Customs*, a setting of Edith Sitwell's frightening poem, for speakers, male chorus and orchestra, was impressive though not quite strong enough in its musical foundation to be entirely convincing. Since then (1949) he has set *The River-run* (James Joyce) for speaker and orchestra, and in 1952, turning again to Edith Sitwell, *The Shadow of Cain.*

ELISABETH LUTYENS also studied both in London, at the Royal College of Music, and abroad, in her case, in Paris. Besides her serious concert music, she has written with much adroitness a fair amount of music for films and for radio features and plays, some of it light in nature and of considerable charm. An example heard in the concert hall is her *Petite Suite,* which Sir Adrian Boult conducted at the Proms in 1947. Throughout her concert music one notes the economy of the writing, evident both in the total length of works, which seldom exceeds fifteen minutes, and in the instrumentation: in this quality she shows the influence of Webern more than Humphrey Searle does. Her ideas are acutely crystallised: there is no inflation or unnecessary busyness. Her most important work is perhaps to be found in her chamber music, which includes three string quartets—the third of which is specially successful, and, being rather easy to follow, serves as a good introduction to her work—and a separate group of three string quartets, all written in 1952 as one opus number. A set of six chamber concertos, all short, for various combinations of wind and strings, are also characteristic of her work and increase the small repertoire of contemporary music for manageable chamber ensembles. She has written relatively less for full orchestra, though her *Three Symphonic Preludes,* performed at the first post-war Festival of the International Society for Contemporary Music held in London in 1946, consistently held one's attention, again being concise and clear-thinking.

Another woman composer, roughly the same age as Miss Lutyens, is ELIZABETH MACONCHY. She also trained at the Royal College of Music and then gained a travelling scholarship to Prague. In the 1930s her works received attention abroad as well as in London, where in 1930 one of her earliest orchestral compositions was performed under Sir Henry Wood at the Proms: this was the suite entitled *The Land,* after the poem by Victoria Sackville-West. She has represented Great Britain several times at the annual festivals of the International Society for Contemporary Music. A good deal of her fairly large output consists of chamber music, and her six string quartets show a positive and forthright personality. She disdains prettiness altogether, and in some of her music she appears to immunise herself against graciousness. In this does she perhaps betray, or compensate for, her femininity? The argument in her music is sternly and often starkly expressed, and the degree of dissonance is not toned down (a movement may sometimes show what amounts to an idiosyncratic obsession with a dissonant interval such as the semitone): but the argument is usually a compelling one that carries the listener along. She has latterly written works of a somewhat lighter nature, such as the entirely effective Concertino for Clarinet and Strings and the Bassoon Concerto, as well as works of warmer character, especially the *Nocturne for Orchestra,* which is one of her best compositions.

If Elizabeth Maconchy's music will be found by some to be too tough meat, the opposite may be said of the work of BENJAMIN FRANKEL. He is, one feels, primarily a gentle and delicate composer, and the character of the music is subtle and elusive, at times almost diffident, rather than immediately striking and forceful. The contrast between his string quartets—there are four—and those of Elizabeth Maconchy is marked: Frankel always works well within the limits of the medium, and these quartets form a body of beautifully written, civilised chamber music, showing a reflective and refined mind. The same may be said of three other chamber works of his, which in date are earlier than the First Quartet: these are a String Trio, a Trio for Clarinet, Cello and Piano, and the likeable un-austere Sonata for Solo Violin (unaccompanied), his only recorded concert work. One of his more important piano works is modestly and appropriately entitled *Sonatina Leggiera,* and is an admirably executed, attractive piece of writing, most playable into the bargain. The quietly imaginative fantasy of the second movement, a three-four *Allegretto,* and the verve of the final *Burlesca*—which characteristically ends softly and not in a display of noisy exuberance—can be picked out as of special appeal. Unimportant, but of much charm, is the group of *Pieces for Geraldine,* also for piano, dedicated to the pianist Geraldine Peppin, and again quite easy to play. As pianists should welcome such grateful music, so string orchestras ought to take to Frankel's suite entitled *Youth Music*. This music is most practically written and light in mood, without being trivial. Attempting little, it is completely successful.

Where Frankel has written works of more ambitious emotional range, such as the Song Cycle to poems of Robert Nichols, entitled *The Aftermath* (1947), or the Violin Concerto of 1951, the result is not always so convincing. However, the implication which may be read into this sentence that Frankel is by nature more suited to smaller-scale work, will quite possibly be entirely disposed of when his First Symphony, on which he is now working, is heard. It remains to be said that Benjamin Frankel is one of the most highly regarded composers of film music in this country. He has written about fifty scores, including those of such outstanding films as *The Importance of Being Earnest, The Man in the White Suit,* and *The Seventh Veil*. His film music cannot be discussed here, but it is far from being a negligible part of his total compositional output, and he has never failed to produce in this medium music of taste, imagination and address. Sometimes a piece from one of his film scores has become deservedly popular: perhaps Frankel's ability to write first-class entertainment music owes a good deal to his early experiences in the music profession. As a young man, studying music in London,[1] he had to supplement the small aid which a scholarship gave him by playing the violin and piano in night clubs. Then he undertook a number of orchestrations for musical comedies, as well as conducting them. It was not long before he gradually managed to get employment in the film studio. Thus his upbringing and entrance into the world of serious music can hardly be said to have been orthodox, but at least it provided him with a much wider technical equipment than the average young composer acquires.

ALAN BUSH, now in his early fifties, occupies a considerable place in English musical life, as composer, teacher, con-

[1] Much of his training was at the Guildhall School of Music, at which he is now a professor of composition.

ductor and organiser, particularly in working-class circles, politically of the Left. It is important to mention this, for he has always openly proclaimed the fact that his musical and his political-sociological ideas are intrinsically bound up with each other. How much real influence the latter have had on his creative side is, however, open to question: on the occasion of his 50th birthday, a collection of tributes to him was compiled,[1] including one from Vaughan Williams, who wrote:

Alan Bush has rather fantastic notions of the nature and purpose of the Fine Arts. Luckily for us when the inspiration comes over him he forgets all about this and remembers only the one eternal rule for all artists—'To thine own self be true'.

Whatever views one may hold on this point, there is no doubt that Alan Bush has given admirable service in helping working-class people towards a greater appreciation and practice of the art of music. In his earlier days he assisted Rutland Boughton as conductor of the London Labour Choral Union, and later, in 1936, he founded the Workers' Music Association, whose choir he conducts, and in whose many other activities he is a tireless mentor.

Alan Bush was trained both at the Royal Academy of Music (where he later returned as a professor of composition, one of his earliest pupils being the late Herbert Murrill) and at the Royal College of Music. Here he was very greatly helped by the counsel of John Ireland. A deep friendship developed between teacher and pupil, and many years later Ireland dedicated to Alan Bush his *These Things Shall Be*.

Bush's own compositions show little influence of his teachers. His work is characterised by contrapuntal and harmonic firmness, and an absence of padding in inner parts, which are usually of thematic significance. Among his prewar output, his *Dialectic* for string quartet, written as early as 1929 and recorded some twenty years later under the auspices of the British Council, is one of his finest compositions, and an outstanding contribution to modern English chamber music. It is both concise and brilliant, and is above

[1] Published by the Workers' Music Association.

all a 'logical disputation'—which is the dictionary meaning of its title. Also dating from before the war is the Concerto for Piano and Orchestra, with baritone solo and male voice chorus, a work of formidable dimensions. Of his more recent compositions, the *Nottingham Symphony,* enterprisingly commissioned in 1949 by the City of Nottingham to celebrate its 500th anniversary, proved to be a rather disappointing work. On the other hand, his Violin Concerto, first performed by Max Rostal, for whom it was written, at a Promenade Concert in the same year, is a masterly composition which we do not hear often enough. On a much simpler level, but an equally distinguished piece of music, is his Christmas cantata, *The Winter Journey,* for soprano and baritone soli and mixed chorus, with text by Randall Swingler. Of particular beauty in this attractive and moving work are the two choruses, 'The Sleepers in the City' and the sustained final chorale, which are much more straightforwardly chordal than is most of Bush's music. It should be mentioned that Alan Bush has written a great number of occasional songs for mixed choir, published by the Workers' Music Association, several with texts also by Randall Swingler. His latest work, still to be given here, is his opera *Wat Tyler,* with libretto by his wife. It is reported that the opera will be first seen in Germany in the autumn of 1953, and it is highly spoken of by those who know the score.

I have left until last the youngest composer discussed in this chapter, or, indeed, in this book: PETER RACINE FRICKER. The rise of this composer in the English musical scene has been little short of spectacular: since 1949 he has had an almost unceasing string of successful performances, capturing the attention of musicians not only in this country but on the continent of Europe, noticeably in Germany. He has also won a number of prizes and awards. No young native composer has achieved renown so rapidly since Britten did in the early 1930s: the two composers in no way resemble one another —only in the fact that both of them, at the very outset of their careers, possessed an absolute and uncannily mature command of technique, are they to be likened to each other. Fricker's training at the Royal College of Music was interrupted by the war years, when he served in the Far East. On demobilisation he continued his studies privately, with the Hungarian composer and teacher resident here since 1935, Mátyás Seiber. To him, Fricker's one-movement String Quartet is dedicated: this was one of the first works to bring its composer before an international audience, when it was played at the Brussels Festival of the International Society for Contemporary Music in 1950. It was already obvious that, in training, outlook and appeal, here once more was a composer to be labelled European rather than English in the localised sense. In the same year, and within a month of that Brussels performance, Fricker had an even more striking success: his First Symphony, which had won a Koussevitsky award, was played at the Cheltenham Festival by the Hallé Orchestra under Barbirolli. The following year saw the production of his Violin Concerto and his Second Symphony, which was commissioned by the City of Liverpool for the Festival of Britain, and first performed there under Hugo Rignold. At the time of writing, a further commissioned work has yet to be heard, a Piano Concerto written for Harriet Cohen. A Viola Concerto for William Primrose, and a Second String Quartet were performed respectively at the Edinburgh and Cheltenham Festivals in 1953. Enough has been said to invalidate the theory that a truly gifted young composer lacks encouragement in our post-war world.

What may be found surprising about Fricker's ascendancy is that his music has no element of popularity in it, has not the vivid shafts of light, which, for example, the early works of Britten and Walton radiated. Fricker's music is difficult to listen to, demanding a considerable degree of concentration from the listener. Its idiom is advanced and uncompromising, often atonal or near-atonal. It is for the most part intensely serious and severely logical. He has been criticised for being too unremittingly serious, too 'grey'. And in certain of the works I have mentioned, the listener may be forgiven for wishing for some relief from the predominantly taut earnestness of the thinking. Yet Fricker has at times shown himself to be capable of relaxation. In the First Symphony there is an immediately attractive movement entitled 'Tableau and Dance', which does not perhaps fit entirely convincingly into the whole work, but is in itself a charmingly written piece. Two excellent works on a slighter scale than the symphonies, and more easily accessible, are the *Prelude, Elegy and Finale* for strings, and the lively, concise and rather Bartókian Concertante for three pianos, strings and percussion (at least the combination is Bartókian). He has shown, too, a lyrical gift in the gentle and relatively simple opening pages of the Violin Concerto, where the solo violin floats an expressive tune high above a sustained accompaniment. In the very slight *Three Songs of Cecco Angiolieri* (a contemporary of Dante) for tenor and seven instruments, there is a dry wit, exceptional in his output so far. Thus the generally intense seriousness, which is at present the salient characteristic of Fricker's music, is tempered by occasional glimpses of other moods, still to be fully realised by their creator. The whole composer has perhaps not yet emerged, his technical maturity is not quite matched by a full emotional range. We are stimulated by his music, even if we find difficulty in loving it. His future development must be watched with the keenest anticipation, for his is unquestionably the most impressive talent to appear in post-war England.

DISCOGRAPHY

This list is not meant to be exhaustive and consists mainly of records currently available in England. (*a*—American recording only.)

I—RALPH VAUGHAN WILLIAMS

Come down, O Love Divine	Templars Octet	HMV. C 3785
Come Holy Spirit, Most Blessed Lord (motet)		
Concerto Accademico (vn. & o.)	St. Paul's Cathedral Choir	Col. LX 1572
	Fuchs, Zimbler Sinfonietta	Brunswick AXTL 1006
	Grinke, Boyd Neel O.	Decca AX248-9
Concerto for ob. & str.	Miller, Saidenberg O.	*a*Mer. Set DM 7 also *a*MG 10003
Concerto for 2 Pf. & o.	Whitemore, Lowe, Robin Hood Dell O.	*a*Vic. LM 135
Fantasia on Greensleeves	New S.O., c. Collins	Decca LXT 2699
,, ,, ,,	Hallé O., c. Sargent	Col. DX 1087
,, ,, ,,	,, c. Barbirolli	HMV. C 3819
,, ,, ,,	Jacques O.	Col. DX 925
Fantasia on a Theme of Tallis	New S.O., c. Collins	Decca LXT 2699
,, ,, ,, ,, ,, ,,	Minneapolis S.O., c. Mitropoulos	*a*Col. ML 4196
,, ,, ,, ,, ,, ,,	Hallé O., c. Barbirolli	HMV. C 3507-8
,, ,, ,, ,, ,, ,,	B.B.C. S.O., c. Boult	HMV. DB 3958-9
,, ,, ,, ,, ,, ,,	B.B.C. S.O., c. Sargent	HMV. DB 9783-4
,, ,, ,, ,, ,, ,,	B.B.C. S.O., c. Sargent	HMV. BLP 1019
Flos Campi	Concert Hall S.O., c. Hull	Nixa CLP 1151
,, ,,	B.B.C. Chorus, Philharmonia O., c. Boult	HMV. DB 6353-5
Folk Song Suite (arr. G. Jacob)	C.B. S.O., c. Barlow	Col. DB 1930-1
For all the Saints	Templars Octet	HMV. C 3784
Forty-Ninth Parallel (film music. Theme from prelude)	L.S.O., c. Mathieson	HMV. B 9879
He who would valiant be	Templars Octet	HMV. C 3783
Hugh the Drover: Song of the Road	Johnston	Col. DX 1668
Job, a Masque for Dancing	B.B.C. S.O., c. Boult	HMV. DB 6829-93
Lark Ascending (vn. & o.)	Grinke, Boyd Neel O.	Decca AX 259-60
	Wise, Liverpool P.O., c. Sargent	Col. DX 1386-7
Linden Lea (song)	McCormack	HMV. DA 1791
	Nash	HMV. B 9719
Lord, Thou hast been our refuge	St. George's Chapel Choir	Col. LX 1390
Loves of Joanna Godden (film music. Excerpts)	Philharmonia O., c. Irving	Col. DX 1377
Mass in G mi.	Fleet Street Choir	Decca LXT 2794
	Fleet Street Choir	Decca AK 1774-6
"Kyrie" only	Westminster Abbey Choir	Col. DB 1786
O Taste and See (motet)	Coronation Service, 1953	HMV. ALP 1056-8
On Wenlock Edge (song cycle)	Pears, Britten, Zorian Qu.	Decca AM 585-7
Orpheus with his Lute (song)	Henderson	Decca M 583
Romance for Harmonica & str. o.	Adler, O., c. Sargent	Col. DX 1861
Scott of the Antarctic (film music. Excerpts)	Philharmonia O., c. Irving	HMV. C 3834
Serenade to Music	16 soloists, B.B.C. Chor. & O., c. Wood	Col. LX 757-8
,, ,, ,,	Royal Festival Hall Chor. & O., c. Boult	HMV. DA 7040-1
Silent Noon (song)	Nash	HMV. C 4210
Song of Thanksgiving	Dolemore, Speaight, Luton C.S., L.P.O., c. Boult	Parl. SW 8138-9

I—RALPH VAUGHAN WILLIAMS—continued

Songs of Travel (song cycle)	Irwin & Moore	HMV. B 9504-5
The Vagabond only	Nash	HMV. C 4210
Suite for Pipes	New Pipers' Guild Quartet	Col. DX 1345
Symphony No. 2 (The London)	L.P.O., c. Boult	Decca LXT 2787
		aLLP 569
	Queen's Hall O., c. Wood	Decca AX 114-8
,, No. 3 (The Pastoral)	L.P.O., c. Boult	Decca LXT 2787
,, No. 5 (D ma.)	Hallé O., c. Barbirolli	HMV. C 3388-92
,, No. 6 (E mi.)	L.S.O., c. Boult	HMV. C 3873-76
,, ,, ,, ,,	L.S.O., c. Boult	HMV. BLP 1001
,, ,, ,,	L.S.O., c. Menges	HMV. C 4195
,, ,, ,,	N.Y.P., c. Stokowski	aCol. ML 4214
Te Deum in F	Coronation Service, 1937	HMV. RG 13-14
Te Deum in G	St. George's Chapel Choir	Col. LX 1289
The Wasps (overture)	Hallé O., c. Sargent	Col. DX 1088
The Water Mill (song)	Evans	Decca K 862
Wither's Rocking (hymn)	School Choir	HMV. C 3525

II—JOHN IRELAND

April, pf. solo	Ireland	HMV. DB 9652
Concertino Pastorale	Boyd Neel O.	Decca AX 253-5
Concerto for pf. & o.	Joyce, Hallé O., c. Heward	Col. DX 1072-4
,, ,, ,,	Mewton-Wood, Utrecht S.O., c. Goehr	aConcert Hall CHS 1167
Downland Suite (minuet)	Boyd Neel O.	Decca AX 255
The Forgotten Rite	Hallé O., c. Barbirolli	HMV. C 3894
The Holy Boy (cello & pf.)	Hooton & Pratt	Decca AK 899
London Overture	Liverpool P. O., c. Sargent	Col. DX 1155-6
Mai Dun	Hallé O., c. Barbirolli	HMV. DB 9651-2
The Overlanders (film music)	L.S.O., c. Mathieson	Decca K 1602
Phantasy Trio in A mi. (No. 1)	Grinke, Hooton, Taylor	Decca AK 899-900
Pianoforte pieces:— Decorations; London Pieces; Sonata	Parkin	Argo RG 4
Sea Fever (song)	Harvey	HMV. B 10233
,, ,,	Henderson	Decca M 526
,, ,,	Irwin	HMV. B 9073
	Robeson	HMV. B 9275
The Soldier (song)	Henderson	Decca M 526
Sonata No. 1 in D mi. (vn. & pf.)	Grinke & Ireland	Decca AK 1400-3
These Things Shall Be (cantata)	Hallé Choir & O., c. Barbirolli	HMV. C 3826-7
Trio No. 3 in E ma.	Grinke, Hooton, Taylor	Decca AX 242-4

III—SIR ARNOLD BAX

Coronation March, 1953	L.S.O., c. Sargent	Decca LXT 2793
Elegiac Trio (for hp., fl., viola)	Ruderman, Thomas, Craft	aAlco. 1007
The Garden of Fand	R.P.O., c. Beecham	HMV. DB 6654-5
I heard a piper (song)	Desmond	Decca M 522
Mater Ora Filium	B.B.C. Chor., c. Woodgate	Eng. Mus. Soc. II
Morning Song, Maytime in Sussex	Cohen, L.S.O., c. Sargent	Col. DX 1838
Nonet for str. qu., fl., ob., clar., & hp.		Eng. Mus. Soc. II
Overture to a Picaresque Comedy	L.P.O., c. Harty	Col. LX 394
Paean (pf. solo)	Cohen	Col. DB 1786
Quartet for str. No. 1 in G	Griller Qu.	Decca AK 1009-12
Quintet for hp. & str.	Newall, Stuyvesant Qu.	aPhil. PH 102
Rann of Exile (song)	Dawson	HMV. B 8866
Royal Wedding Fanfares		HMV. B 9616
Sonata for viola & hp.	Forbes & Korchinska	Decca AK 941-3
,, ,, viola & pf.	Primrose & Cohen	Eng. Mus. Soc. II
Symphony No. 3	Hallé O., c. Barbirolli	HMV. C 3380-5
The White Peace (song)	McCormack, Moore	HMV. DA 1791

IV—SIR ARTHUR BLISS

Checkmate (ballet)	Royal Opera O., c. Irving	Col. DX 1718-20
		*a*Col. ML 362
Concerto for pf & o.	Solomon," Liverpool P.O., c. Boult	HMV. C 3348-52
„ „ „	Mewton-Wood, Winterthur S.O., c. Goehr	Nixa CLP 1167
Fanfare Jubilante, etc.	Royal Mil. Sch.	HMV. B 9616
Men of Two Worlds (film music)	Baraza. Joyce, N.S.O., c. Mathieson	Decca K 1174
Miracle in the Gorbals (ballet)	Royal Opera O., c. Lambert	*a*Col. ML 2117
Pastoral	Evans, Morris, Taylor, B.B.C. Chor., Jacques S.O.	Decca AX 564-7
Phoenix March	Philharmonia O., c. Lambert	HMV. C 3518
Polonaise (pf. solo)	Smith	Decca K 780
Quartet for str., in B flat	Griller Qu.	Decca AK 1091-4
„ „ „ *No. 2 in F mi.*	Griller Qu.	Decca LX 3038
Quintet for cl. & str.	Thurston & Griller Qu.	Decca AK 780-3
Sonata for viola & pf.	Forbes & Foggin	Decca AX 233-5
Things to Come (film music)	L.S.O., c. Bliss	Decca K 810-11
„ „ „	„ c. Mathieson	Decca K 817

V—ARTHUR BENJAMIN

Carribean Dance	Smith, Sellick	Col. DB 2558
	New Concert O., c. Robinson	BH. 02093
Fanfare for a festive occasion	Royal Mil. Sch.	HMV. B 9616
From San Domingo	New Concert O., c. Robinson	BH. O 2093
Jamaican Rumba	New Concert O., c. Robinson	BH. O 2056
	Smith, Sellick	Col. DX 1555
Mattie Rag „	Smith, Sellick	Col. DX 1555
	New Concert O., c. Robinson	BH. O 2056
Overture „to an Italian Comedy	New Concert O., c. Robinson	BH. O 2080
	Chicago S.O., c. Stock	HMV. ED 282
Red „*River Jig* „ „	New Concert O., c. Robinson	BH. O 2147
Concerto for oboe and strings (Cimarosa-Benjamin)	Goossens, Liverpool P.O., c. Sargent	Col. DX 1137-8

VI—E. J. MOERAN

Symphony in G mi.	Hallé O., c. Heward	HMV. C 3319-24

VII—GORDON JACOB

No records available

VIII—EDMUND RUBBRA

Improvisation (Op. 50, No. 4) on Farnaby's *Loth to Depart*	Hallé O., c. Barbirolli	HMV. DB 21387
Missa in Honorem S. Dominici, Op. 66	Fleet Str. Choir	Decca LXT 2794
Quartet for str. No. 2 in E flat	Griller Qu.	Decca LX 3088
	Griller Qu.	*a*LPS 657
Sonata No. 2, „ Op. „ 31, „ for vn. & pf.	Sammons & Moore	HMV. C 3547-8
Symphony No. 5 in B flat, Op. 63	Hallé O., c. Barbirolli	HMV. DB 21384-7
	Hallé O., c. Barbirolli	BLP. 1021
Trio „ *for pf., vn.* „ *& cello* „	Rubbra, Gruenberg, Pleeth	Argo RG 5

IX—SIR WILLIAM WALTON

Belshazzar's Feast	Huddersfield Choral Soc., Liverpool P.O., c. Walton	HMV. C 3330-34
Concerto for Violin	Heifetz, Philharmonia O., c. Walton	HMV. DB 21257-9
„ „ „	Heifetz, Philharmonia O., c. Walton	*a*Vic. LM 1121

IX—Sir William Walton—*continued*

Concerto for Viola	Primrose, Philharmonia O., c. Walton	HMV. DB 6309-11
	Riddle, L.S.O., c. Walton	Decca AX 199-201
Coronation Marches (Crown Imperial: Orb and Sceptre)	Philharmonia O., c. Walton	Col. 33C 1016
	L.S.O., c. Sargent	Decca LXT 2793
Coronation Marches (Crown Imperial only)	B.B.C. S.O., c. Boult	HMV. DB 3164
Coronation Marches (Orb and Sceptre only)	Philharmonia O., c. Walton	Col. LX 1583
Façade (original version)	Sitwell, Lambert, O.	aCol. ML 2047
		Decca K 991-2
Façade (Suite for orch.)	Philharmonia O., c. Lambert	Col. 33SX 1003
		Col. DX 1734-6
" "	L.S.O., c. Irving	Decca LXT 2791
	L.P.O., c. Walton	HMV. C 2836-7
Hamlet (film music)	Philharmonia O., c Mathieson	HMV. C 3735-7
Henry V (film music)	Philharmonia O., c. Walton	HMV. C 3583-6
Portsmouth Point (overture)	Philharmonia O., c. Walton	Col. 33C 1016
Quartet in A mi., for str.	Hollywood Qu.	Capitol CTL 7004
	Hollywood Qu.	aCapitol P 8054
Quartet for pf. & str.	Paul Qu.	Decca AX 238-41
Scapino (overture)	Philharmonia O., c. Walton	HMV. DB 21499
	Chicago S.O., c. Stock	Col. LX 931
Sinfonia Concertante for pf & orch.	Sellick, Birmingham S.O., c. Weldon	HMV. C 7635-7
Sonata for vn & pf.	Menuhin, Kentner	HMV. DB 9512-5
Spitfire Prelude & Fugue	Hallé O., c. Walton	HMV. C 3359
Symphony	L.S.O., c. Harty	Decca AX 108-13
	Philharmonia O., c. Walton	HMV. ALP 1027
Where does the uttered music go?	B.B.C. Chorus, c. Walton	HMV. C 3503

X—LENNOX BERKELEY

Divertimento in B flat	L.C.O., c. Bernard	Decca AK 1882-3
Preludes (6) for pf. solo	Horsley	HMV. C 3940

XI—MICHAEL TIPPETT

Boyhood's End (song cycle)	Pears, Mewton-Wood	Argo RG 15
Concerto for Double Str. Orch.	Philharmonia O., c. Goehr	HMV. C 7926-8
Fantasy Sonata (for pf.)	Sellick	RVW. 108/10S
Heart's Assurance (song cycle)	Pears, Mewton-Wood	Argo RG 15
Quartet for str. No. 2 in F sharp mi.	Zorian Qu.	Decca AK 1925-7

XII—ALAN RAWSTHORNE

Bagatelles (4) for pf. solo	Matthews	HMV. C 3324
Concerto No. 2 for pf.	Curzon, L.S.O., c. Sargent	Decca LX 3066
		aLPS 513
French Nursery Songs (3)	Wyss " "	Decca K 1065
Street Corner Overture	Philharmonia O., c. Lambert	HMV. C 3502
Symphonic Studies, 1939	Philharmonia O., c. Lambert	HMV. C 3542-4
Theme & Variations for str. qu.	Hirsch Qu.	Argo RG 3
Theme & Variations for 2 vns.	Washbourne, Hinchcliffe	Decca AK 884-5

XIII—CONSTANT LAMBERT

Horoscope (ballet)	L.S.O., c. Irving	Decca LXT 2791
"	Philharmonia O., c. Lambert	Col. DX 1196-7
		DX 1567-8
"	" " "	Col. 33SX 1003
		aCol. ML 2083
Rio Grande	Greenbaum, Philharmonia O., c. Lambert	Col. DX 1591-2
		Col. 33SX 1003
		aCol. ML 2145

XIV—HERBERT MURRILL

No records available

XV—BENJAMIN BRITTEN

Abraham & Isaac—Canticle No. 2 Op. 51	Pears, Ferrier, acc. Britten	Decca LXT 2789
The Birds (song)	Neely	HMV. B 10041
Ceremony of Carols, Op. 28	Washington Cath. Choir	aWCFM 11
	Morriston Boys Choir	Decca AK 1155-7
Fantasy for ob. & str.	Gomberg, Galimer Qu.	aEsoteric 504
Folk Song Arrangements	Pears, Britten	HMV. 7 R 108
,, ,, ,,	,, ,,	Decca M 555
,, ,, ,,	,, ,,	HMV. DA 1873
,, ,, ,,	Schiötz	HMV. X 8009
	Wyss	Decca M 568
Holy Sonnets of John Donne, Op. 35	Pears, Britten	HMV. DB 6689-91
Hymn to St. Cecilia, Op. 27	Fleet Str. Choir	Decca AK 1088-9
	Washington Cath. Choir	aWCFM 11
Les Illuminations, Op. 18	Mock, La Jalla O., c. Sokoloff	aAlco Y 1211
Introduction & Rondo Alla Burlesca, Op. 23, No. 1 for 2 pfs.	Curzon, Britten	Decca K 1117
Mazurka Elegiaca, Op. 23, No. 2 for 2 pfs.	Curzon, Britten	Decca K 1118
Michelangelo Sonnets (7)	Pears, Britten	HMV B 9302 & C 3312
Peter Grimes (opera), Op. 33. Sea Interludes	L.S.O., c. Sargent	Col. DX 1441-2
Peter Grimes, Sea Interludes (& Passacaglia)	Concertgebouw O., c. van Beinum	Decca AK 1702-4
Quartet for str., No. 1 in D, Op. 25	Griller Qu.	aEsoteric 504
Quartet for str. No. 2 in C, Op. 36	Zorian Qu.	HMV. C 7651-4
The Rape of Lucretia (opera), Op. 37 (Abridged version)	c. Goodall	HMV. C 3699-3706
Rejoice in the Lamb (cantata) Op. 30	Nat. Presb. Choir	aWCFM. LP 4
Serenade for tenor, hn., & str. Op. 31	Pears, Brain, Boyd Neel O., c. Britten	Decca AK 1151-3
Simple Symphony, Op. 4	Boyd Neel O.	Decca AX 245-7
Soirees Musicales, Op. 9 (Rossini-Britten)	C. Brill O.	Decca AK 873-4
Te Deum, Op. 32	Washington Cath. Choir	aWCFM 11
Variations on a Theme of Frank Bridge	Boyd Neel O.	Decca LXT 2790 AK 2307-9
Village Harvest (Irish Reel)	C. Brill O.	Decca K 874
Young Person's Guide to the Orchestra, Op. 34	Liverpool P.O., c. Sargent	Col. DX 1307-8 & DXS 1309 aCol. ML 4197

XVI—MISCELLANEOUS COMPOSERS

(a) HUMPHREY SEARLE

Sonata for pf.	Watson	Argo RG 6

(d) BENJAMIN FRANKEL

Sonata for unacc. violin, Op. 13	Rostal	Decca AK 1178-9

(e) ALAN BUSH

Dialectic, for str. qu.	Aeolian Qu.	Decca AK 1852-4

(f) PETER RACINE FRICKER

Sonata for vn. & pf.	Lidka, Kitchin	Argo RG 7

DATE DUE

GAYLORD   PRINTED IN U.S.A.